The Street of Good Fortune

The Street of Good Fortune

Maryam Manteghi

Forefront Media Group

THE STREET OF GOOD FORTUNE Copyright © 2014 Maryam Manteghi

First edition published by Forefront Media Group PTY Ltd., 2014
www.forefrontmedia.co.za

All rights reserved. No part of this publication may be reproduced, stored in a retrieval system, or transmitted, in any form or by any means electronic, mechanical, photocopying, recording or otherwise without the prior permission of the publisher.

Cover art by Sana Mohtadi - Cover design by Leyla T. Haidarian
ISBN: 0615970710
ISBN: 9780615970714
www.thestreetofgoodfortune.com

To Beks, my sister in sickness and in health

Acknowledgments

I WROTE THIS book as an homage to the country and the people who inspired me. I returned to my home in Canada from a six year sojourn in Bosnia and Herzegovina in 2007 and often felt that my years in Bosnia had been a dream. That they had only ever happened in my head. As I lived a daily life completely removed from the life I'd had in Sarajevo, Bosnia's capital, I desperately felt the need to secure my six years there in some permanent way before the magic of that time faded. I couldn't bear to forget the place I had fought so hard not to leave and where I had become somebody nobody in Canada could understand. I hope that I was able to do justice to that magic.

Of course I can't escape the fact that I also wrote this book as a way of dealing with the enemy in my breast that forced me back to Canada, back to my home and the place of my exile. I wrote to somehow heal myself, to give meaning to the time spent in hospitals and bald while I felt everyone around me was living lives brimming with achievement and success. My chapters almost always include a sliver or more of pity for myself with a memory of life in Bosnia as a way of giving myself perspective during the pain I was feeling at the time. Self-pity is very un-Bosnian and through writing I empowered myself to stop feeling it.

The process of writing this book was one of the most joyous and exciting periods of my life in which many people participated whether they know it or not and to whom I am indebted.

There is no chronological order to gratitude and yet I feel that my first line of thanks must be to my editor Fraser Sutherland. When a bearded, Scottish poet tells you that your writing is remarkable, you feel like you can do anything. His ability to shape my wild undirected thoughts into something so much more is the reason there is a book at all. His kind, gentle manner and his fierce intelligence inspired and guided me through the pages and chapters and, to me, he will forever be the hero of this book and any other book I ever write.

To the army of friends and family who tirelessly read, re-read and revised the book and took my writing beyond the limits of my comfort zone, I can only say that without your input I would not be here writing this. Thank you Nava Beheshti Sarooshi for always giving me your truly undivided time, attention and infallible attention to detail. Thanks to Jackie Rudberg for the hours and hours of analysis and over-analysis and for standing next to me in chemo and in writing; always loyal and beautiful. Thanks to Saghar Maani for being possibly the only person in the world who thinks exactly like I do and who opened the door to this wonderful journey.

Thanks to Maryam Mazgani who insisted on better business practices and who believed that I was worth more than I thought. You always have my back like nobody else. Thanks to Mahsa Merrikh Firoozmand for her unbiased opinions on the chapters and for her support. Thanks to Lids for being my most well-connected friend and my lucky charm. Thanks to my beautiful cousin Sana Mohtadi for her gorgeous artwork that adorns the cover and her matter of fact conclusion of "It makes me want to go to Sarajevo" when she finished her first read. That is exactly what I wanted to hear. Thanks to my precious uncle Riaz Masrour, an incredibly talented writer and scholar of Baha'i history whose encouragement and support I cherish. Thanks to Olivera Markovic and Almira Pozder for everything that words cannot adequately express. Thanks to Leyla Tavernaro Haidarian for her vision, her faith and her friendship. I wouldn't want to be anywhere else.

To my parents who insisted on private schools and Persian classes, I hope that I've made you proud.

To Marwan Al Chamaa, the man who saw me and my writing as one and married both of us. I can only say that I can't write what is beyond words.

And to the country of my heart my own words will not do:

MARYAM MANTEGHI

"This is the kind of Friend
You are —
Without making me realize
My soul's anguished history,
You slip into my house at night,
And while I am sleeping,
You silently carry off
All my suffering and sordid past
In Your beautiful
Hands."
-Hafiz

Maryam Manteghi

Contents

Acknowledgments vii
One **Don't Worry, We Have A Binder** 1
Two **Christiane Amanpour, Meet Kylie Minogue** · 13
Three **They Found My Genes On College Street** · · 33
Four **A Tree Grows in Oakville
     Except It's Not an Oak** 51
Five **It Happened in the Shower** 65
Six **Peeing Red** 73
Seven **No Homes and No Families** 91
Eight **I Have A Scar, A Big Scar Across
     My Left Breast** 111
Nine **This Was the Man-Boy** 137
Ten **An Iranian in Bosnia** 159
Eleven **"Meri, Can I Call You Mama?"** 173
About the Author 197

1

Don't Worry, We Have a Binder

Though hair does grow back, ovaries do not. I didn't cry when the surgeon told me I had cancer. Mostly because I was in shock but also perhaps deep down I somehow sensed not so much that I was sick, more that I was about to face a test unlike any I had faced before. I didn't cry when my boyfriend of five years, the younger Man-Boy I planned to marry, broke up with me over the phone the night before I started chemo. I didn't even cry when I realised that I was not going back to my Sarajevo, the only place in the world I'd ever felt truly at home, not for a very long time. I did cry, though, when Dr. Verma explained that the chemo I would receive might leave me unable to have children. I fell into his arms and sobbed uncontrollably till I couldn't breathe and Dr. Verma's white coat had my bodily fluids all over it. He didn't move until I stopped crying. My reaction, I think, surprised me more than anyone else. Suddenly, all the things that I had taken for granted would simply happen were being snatched away from me.

I suddenly felt like I was being punished for not having the foresight to plan a normal life. An ordinary life that in a split second had become extraordinary. The same kind of life that I escaped when I left in 2002 on a one-way flight to Sarajevo. The same life that I was so relieved not to be living when I saw my friends tied to houses, children, nannies, minivans, and the mundane everydayness of suburban life.

Until now.

Punished for having made different choices than my peers. Punished for living a life where I never thought about mortgages and families and job security. Sitting there sobbing on Dr. Verma's white lab coat, I wondered why I had never thought about those things. How had I missed entire chunks of life that had occupied my friends during the last five years? What was I doing when they were all getting engaged, buying houses and planning babies? How was it that I had never, until this day, sitting in a Sunnybrook Hospital examination room in Toronto, seriously concerned myself with the business of family and children? It wasn't that I didn't want children or a family, it was just that I always thought that marriage and children simply happened to people and that they would simply just happen to me too at some faraway point. And even this thought was at the back of my mind. The front of my mind had always been occupied with more current events. Like today, or tomorrow or, at most, next week.

My immediate reaction was to blame my parents. Why didn't they tell me? Why didn't they, like normal immigrant families, become alarmed when their only daughter wasn't married at 30? Why didn't they nag me about being grandparents or put out a public call to our substantial network of friends, family and acquaintances to drum up some suitable men? Where was the team of middle-aged women in my community whose job it was to make matches? I mean I was an IRANIAN. Hello? Matchmakers, setups, Yenta characters straight out of *Fiddler on the Roof*. How had I fallen through the cracks?

As I lamented the state of my non-union and allowed myself to swim in self-pity, my rational brain took over. Despite my law degree, my rational brain only takes over when truth knocks desperately at the door and I pretend not to hear it. Thankfully, rational brain opened the door and truth walked in: five-and-a-half years of memories that, like a series of movie trailers, answered all my questions in a single sentence:

I had been living my dream. My Christiane Amanpour Balkan dream.

And for a split second another thought flashed through my head. If they, whoever they were, told me to give those years back, in return for not getting breast cancer, for not being at Sunnybrook sobbing on Dr. Verma, for not facing this journey ahead of me, I would say no.

My mother and I were sitting in an Elm Street vegetarian restaurant when I got a call from Dr. Verma. It had been about a week since I'd been diagnosed and I was still in a daze.

"So, Maryam, do you have a partner?"

Did I have a partner? My brain suddenly shuffled back to the commercial ideas I had come up with in Sarajevo and the business partners with whom I discussed them. How did Dr. Verma know about that? How intuitive of him, I thought, and then I realised that he actually meant life partner.

Boyfriend.

Significant other of opposite sex.

Really, he was asking me if I had a man.

More specifically, a man with sperm he could offer to the cause.

He was talking about fertility treatments, the possibility which he and his nurse Tammy offered me when it was clear that I was to undergo eight rounds of chemotherapy after which I might not be able to have kids. Fertility treatments, they said, could harvest my eggs and, if necessary, make it possible for me to conceive in vitro. I had a fuzzy idea what this meant. I knew that Celine Dion had to do that because her husband was about a hundred years old. I'd also read somewhere that Kylie Minogue had had her eggs frozen and that consoled me to a certain extent. This might be OK. Kylie didn't have a man either. The slimy French actor that she'd been dating during chemo dumped her after treatment. Kylie and I could have babies at the same time! If I were going to harvest my eggs, it would have to be done immediately. I couldn't start chemo until the eggs were harvested and Dr. Verma wanted me to start chemo, like, yesterday. I agreed to an appointment at the fertility clinic at Mount Sinai Hospital.

It was a beautiful, sunny day as my mother and I walked up the steps into Mount Sinai. My mother had a distinctly pissed-off look on her face. She was not sharing my sudden obsession with babies. For me, babies represented a world in which I was being denied citizenship; a world to which I had a free pass until very recently. A world my friends and women all around me seemingly effortlessly inhabited. A world of Baby Gap and Gymboree, of designer strollers with Italian names, of Whole Foods bags and SUVs with baby-on-board signs, car seats and portable DVD players. A world that used to give me panic attacks when I thought of myself in it.

Not anymore.

This world had, over the last few days, become desirable to the point of desperation. As I got reacquainted with Oakville, the upper-crusty Toronto suburb where I grew up, I envied the chic, LuluLemon-clad mommies at Starbucks, with their Tiffany engagement rings and Chicco strollers. I envied their tired looks and trendy Birkenstocks and, most of all, I envied the best-dressed babies they carried on their hips as they ordered decaf, non-fat lattes and blueberry bars. Some of them I recognised as my high-school colleagues and some of them I'd gone to ballet with, but none of them seemed to be aware of how lucky they were. How randomly it could have been otherwise for them. As we entered the clinic, I felt cold. An eerie place where I could swear all the secretaries were pregnant (I suspected being pregnant was one of the criteria for being hired.) In a large waiting room I saw couples; it seemed to me that the women looked worried while the men looked bored. I didn't blame them. I wondered if I had stumbled into a new dimension and if I'd be able to get back out. Thankfully, my mother was there and, believe me, you cannot keep my mother in any dimension against her will. So we sat and waited until a pregnant secretary called our names and we walked past pictures of babies and women with bulging stomachs until we reached the doctor's office.

We entered a cold, bare room that looked like a lawyer's office with diplomas and certificates hanging on the wall. My mother and I sat while, across from us, leaning against a cabinet, a female resident described how this procedure would be carried out with a flip board of diagrams that horrified my mother so much she hissed in Farsi, "*Pasho* (get up)". "*Dare harf mizaneh* (she's talking)," I muttered under my breath as I feigned interest while attempting, unsuccessfully, to veil my own horror at the instrument that was inserted into a diagrammed vagina. It seemed impossible that such a thing could fit in there and yet, there she was, the 12-year-old resident with her pitch perfectly memorised, expressionless as she described horrible, painful things to the point that I wondered if she had a vagina. If she did, she had certainly blocked any possible connection it may have ever had to her feelings. Her über-technical description of the procedure made my teeth hurt and I crossed my legs tightly, attempting to protect my still-intact reproductive organs from the state of deep freeze that seemed to have afflicted her. "The treatments might make the cancer grow or spread but hopefully the chemo will take care of that if it happens," she continued in a monotone. My mother sucked in her breath and gave the child-resident The Look. Among the maternal repertoire of Looks, some of which are not maternal in any way, but were developed by our ancestors to ward off beasts of prey from the nest, this one was the one reserved for a herd of hungry hyenas. It was, incidentally, also the look I received the time I left the kettle on the stove and burned down the kitchen. I hadn't seen it in years and it was bad.

Very bad.

"We're leaving," my mother said in a voice that could cut glass. She got up.

"Ah, um, why don't you wait to see the doctor?" the resident said, suddenly flustered and turning red. "She's coming now," she stuttered. At that point a very pregnant but menopausal-looking doctor entered, belly first, swaying slightly until she was facing us across the desk. She lisped and seemed, like everyone else, disconnected from any emotion, hers or ours. She proceeded to repeat everything the resident had already told us but added, "The treatment costs $10,000 per round. You might need several rounds as the sperm and egg may not actually take the first time. Do you have a partner?"

"Um… he's in Bosnia," I responded weakly.

"Oh, don't worry, we have a binder."

I didn't understand. What did a binder have to do with anything? A nurse brought one in and handed it to us. As we flipped through the pages I, usually painfully naïve, clicked in.

It was a binder of sperm donors.

Every page described a donor from his physical appearance to his blood type and ethnic background. I had no time to think anything. My mother closed the binder, fuming, threw it at the robotic fertility experts and exploded.

"WHAT KIND OF PLACE IS THIS?"

I braced myself for more.

"MY DAUGHTER HAS CANCER AND YOU GIVE US A SPERM BINDER? ARE YOU ALL *CRAZY*? MY DAUGHTER HAS TO LIVE BEFORE SHE HAS BABIES!"

"And I am not paying for this session," she said, much calmer.

Nobody seemed fazed. The pregnant doctor followed us out. "We understand this is a difficult time, why don't you talk to the social worker to help you deal with it all," she called out from behind us. Disoriented, I lost my sense of direction in the vortex of hallways that led out of the clinic's inner sanctum but my mother grabbed my arm and led me out. I saw the social worker try to follow us but my mother whirled around and gave her the look that turned Lot's wife into a pillar of salt. Undaunted, she didn't refrain from calling us every day at 11 am to leave a message for us to call her back to discuss "my options" until one day my mother actually picked up the phone and gave her the option of a harassment claim against the clinic. She never called again.

The baby question haunted me all through my treatment. It became, oddly enough, the single, largest worry I had even as I trudged my clinically-trialled body to bi-monthly chemo treatments and contemplated a possible mastectomy. It manifested itself in a million tiny daily occurrences. I became paralysed every time I saw a feminine hygiene commercial. In fact, formula commercials, diaper commercials, and any commercials with babies, Always with wings, or Midol gave me anxiety attacks. So much so that I actually had to stop watching mainstream television including the Food Channel, which had been the only solace during my ravenous, pumped-up-on-steroids period: where they give you steroids to make sure you eat, even though your body would much rather be hurling all the contents of chemotherapy. Apparently steroid dosages were hard to tweak because I thought about food as many times a day as a 16-year-old boy thinks about sex, constantly ravenous in a primal, prey-seeking sort of way, a cancerorus rex.

I spent much of my chemo couch time watching Iranian satellite television just to avoid the Always commercials on the Food Network. Watching the blue liquid being poured out onto the pads with wings, the ones I used to use, was too much for me to handle. I kept a pack of Always with wings in the bathroom and, despite the fact that I stopped getting my period after the second round of chemo, I held onto that package for dear life, vowing that a day would come when I would use them again. For about a year and a half the one and only prayer that I desperately whispered to my pillow every night was: God, just please let me have my period back. Getting my period back became an end in itself independent of the ability to have children. I figured that as long as I could get my period back, the find-a-mate-and-have-children part would be a snap. But also I longed to be normal again. I longed to become the person I had been before my disease. I compared everything to the old me. I thought of it mostly in physical terms: to have my period back, to have my long hair back, to look like I did before.

I also aspired to go back to being the same person in my head as I had been before I got sick. Even as I felt this, I couldn't understand why this was the case. I mean, hadn't that person been the one to get sick? Obviously she had been doing something fundamentally wrong to end up with locally advanced breast cancer at age 34. Why would I possibly want to go back to being her? After a year of chemo, radiation, and a lumpectomy, which I thought for some months would be a double mastectomy, I felt defeated. I was raw and vulnerable and I stopped trusting myself. The way I saw it was that if I had brought myself, even unwittingly, to the point of near-total destruction, every choice I had ever made had been wrong. I compared myself to my friends and peers. While I was wondering when my eyebrows were going to grow back and how I would wean myself from weekly visits with Dr. Verma, they were living lives straight out of an Ikea catalogue. As much as regular and normal were words I never wished upon myself, my chosen odyssey had ended at the door of Sunnybrook's

Odette Cancer Centre. I had, in following my dream, led myself astray. I felt lost. Unable to make the smallest decisions about my life, I willingly gave up that responsibility to my parents and friends.

The old me had never felt that way. The old me was brave and confident and never afraid to take a risk. The old me lived by her own terms and didn't give a damn what anyone thought. The old me got on a plane the day after being called to the Bar of Ontario to become a full-fledged attorney and flew away from successful career options in her First World country to a post-war transition zone, taking one suitcase and a dream.

The old me was untouchable.

2

CHRISTIANE AMANPOUR, MEET KYLIE MINOGUE

I WAS DIAGNOSED with "The C" on May 10, 2007, my mother's birthday. My mother couldn't bring herself to say "cancer" so in our house it was just called The C as if giving it an alias would somehow trick the disease into having an identity crisis and turning into a common cold or mild constipation.

Don't worry. This will not be the diary of a cancer patient.

Mostly because I was completely turned off by cancer diaries while I was living my own. I tried to read them and browsed the bookstores to see if any of them could make me feel better. I'd open each book, eager to read a page or even a line in which I could find myself, but try as I might, I just couldn't relate to the blow-by-blow, insomnia-curing diaries of Toronto's quasi-celebrity women with kids, careers, doting husbands, and a new lease on middle age since surviving The C.

Maybe if Kylie Minogue had written a cancer diary it might have been different. Diagnosed with The C at the height of her "Showgirl" tour, 36, childless, with a slimy boyfriend that jilted her after chemo, Kylie was me — except blonde, rich, and famous. I searched the Internet for hours on end to see pictures of her during various phases of C-treatment. There were pictures of her during chemo looking very Audrey Hepburn, wearing a stylish scarf and big, big sunglasses topping a waif-like figure in cute little shift dresses. I tried in vain to achieve the KylieChemo look, spending hours in the designer eyewear section at Holt Renfrew, Toronto's poshest department store, trying on sunglasses that cost more than a car in the country I'd just left, Sadly, the bloating from the steroids and the fact that Kylie was, well, Kylie for a reason didn't permit it. After several days of my walking around in bejewelled Dior aviators, my father, whose credit card had suffered the blow of my attempt at KylieChic, broke down and told me that not only did I in no way resemble Kylie, but that I'd perfected a frumpish look with, topping the aviators, a kerchief wrapped around my head like Lawrence of Arabia. The Dior aviators were returned to a Holt Renfrew employee who, from under blue-tipped black bangs, glared at my father while assuring me that they'd looked "fabulous".

During the dirty war that is chemotherapy, I often renewed my will to live by poring over pictures of post-chemo Kylie's cute pixie cut and very successful reconstructive surgery that allowed her to pose on billboards in a silver lamé bikini, like the one I stared at with anticipation and dread when my father drove me downtown for my appointments with Dr. McCready, the reigning god of breast cancer surgery and the man responsible for whether or not a silver lamé bikini could be in *my* future. There were also pictures of post-C Kylie lying provocatively on a piano with a tumble of blonde curls à la Madonna circa *Vogue* cascading over the edge of the instrument that kept my hopes up during my peach fuzz and GI Jane hairstyle periods respectively. Kylie made me feel that bad luck with men and not so great luck with health hadn't just suddenly afflicted me; that I had not been singled out as some cosmic loser. If Kylie and I had the same finger pointing at us, I was OK with that. During those first months of my battle with The C, Kylie was the only woman in the world who I was sure could understand me. Had Kylie had a mastectomy? I wondered desperately when Dr. Verma told me that after chemo, a mastectomy of my breast was the "protocol" in my treatment. How had Kylie felt when they told her they would be cutting off her breast? The sex kitten who'd shot to fame gyrating through her "Spinning Around" video in shiny gold hot pants that left nothing to the imagination — how had she felt when they told her she'd be going from babe to breastless and possibly barren? I consoled myself in my silent conversations with an imaginary Kylie. It must have been so much worse for her, I thought, having built an identity as a pop princess, making a steamy lingerie commercial explicit enough to be banned. I stared at that commercial, the sensual, busty Kylie riding a velvet pony, all bedroom hair and bedroom eyes with her creamy white cleavage amplified in a lacy silk bra. I played and replayed YouTube videos of Kylie in her silver lamé bikini, stepping out of a pool and lying on a towel while I tried to detect which breast had been sliced off, then reconstructed, and told myself that if Kylie could do it, so could I. If 2007 was the year of Kylie's post-cancer, post-loser boyfriend comeback complete with pixie cut and metallic bikini, then one day I too would have a comeback, the when and the how being less important than my unwavering belief that it would happen.

It wasn't the first time I'd channelled a celebrity. The years before my collision with The C, my official celebrity wannabe had about as little in common with Kylie as possible. My girlhood hero was a half-Iranian, fully kick-ass female war correspondent whose wardrobe consisted primarily of bullet proof vests and nerves of steel. Christiane Amanpour would surely have been offended to know that her competition for my affections was a pop princess with a funny accent but, despite the years I'd spent in awe of Christiane as she dodged bullets in Sarajevo's sniper alley and made no apologies for her haircut, Kylie *forcemment* replaced her as my hero. I'd planned to follow in Christiane's footsteps, fearless in khakis, poised, self-assured, and the proud owner of a set of balls most men would envy, all the way through to her sunny Italian wedding to enviable, hot, Jewish bachelor at 39 with just enough window of opportunity to ensure that her still functioning ovaries produced a male heir. Overnight though, my psyche made a paradigm shift to perky Australian singer with a weakness for bad boys and hot pants ambushed at 36 by breast cancer. I was forced to leave CNN's most famous employee in the fairy dust of the enchanted life in which it had all worked out for her. It was fairy dust that had evaded me. Part of me began to resent her and what she represented, this lie that things worked out, that hard work and courage and taking the road less travelled guaranteed success, fame and happiness.

The Street of Good Fortune

Or at least a life without cancer.

I had never aspired to the HGTV version of a perfect life, dismissing those women who bounded into their twenties obsessed with getting the ring, planning the wedding, and renovating the basement of a three-storey, four-bedroom detached dream house on a green, leafy street in the Greater Toronto Area, all to be done right before they started "trying". I could hear them saying: "We're trying for a second baby". They could have just as easily said, "I'm trying to get this stain out" or "I'm trying to get this recipe right". It made me want to laugh out loud. It was so trivial, so self-obsessed. Excuse me, I thought, but I'm trying to drink my cappuccino while thinking great humanitarian thoughts and then I'll be off trying to save the world. I blanked out those women of a certain class, from a certain background, whose task-oriented focus was making sure to tick off all the appropriate boxes on the to-do list of the perfect life: Career? Check. Husband? Check. Showhouse? Check. Baby #1? Check. Baby #2? Check. Finding their life's purpose in fulfilling the necessary criteria to create the illusionary perfect life, proof of which could be found in carefully crafted Facebook photo albums portraying pictures of babies, toddlers and children complete with captions like "Little Mia discovers her toes!"

Let those women have their wedding cake and eat it too, I thought. They weren't biting into my dreams. "Don't become like that," my father would tell me as we sat in cafés watching Oakville mommies stroll around the square. "*Zan va zayeman* (Yuck)," in Farsi, he would mutter in disgust. Further translation: Do not tie yourself down to your reproductive system.

"It's so weird," my friend Dina would say, "he treats you like you're a son". I never thought about it that way but I guess she was right. While Dina's father nearly gave himself a stroke when he was convinced that she, at 31, would never marry and have children, my father viewed such a step as a cop-out. "Don't you want grandchildren?" I would ask him. He looked at me like I had just failed my Grade 9 math exam. Giving birth and all it entailed was not considered an achievement by my father. In a way, I couldn't blame him. Raised in a country where most women had few choices, where marriage and children robbed them of the opportunities and possibilities I took for granted, and where motherhood was a precarious business making a woman dependent on the goodwill of the men in her life, some of my father's perspective seeped into my being.

But did this all mean that I should be punished? Wasn't it every woman's prerogative to change her mind? I knew I couldn't have my cake and eat it too but surely someone could have saved me some icing?

As time went by, I got used to my new status as a C patient, which basically meant that my plans, thoughts and dreams were in suspended reality until such time as this would all be over. I was suddenly devoid of any responsibility other than living.

As in, staying alive.

On the bright side, though, a great weight had been lifted from my shoulders. A friend described to me how she'd decided to think positively despite having, as she herself called it, "a touch of the anorexia", as if it were the 24-hour stomach flu. True, I had a touch of The C, requiring some pretty drastic and intense experiences to neutralise, but other than that, I had no job, didn't need to look for a job, and had no dependants. Nobody expected anything from me other than to wake up in the morning and take an evening stroll at dusk around our little crescent. The usual debilitating societal stresses for a single girl my age suddenly became absurd. Despite my trying circumstances, I was liberated from the myriad of what I considered the superficial expectations of the society I had managed to escape. Nobody asked me when I would be getting married, or if I wanted to meet their cousin's nephew who was an engineer but now owned a very successful jewellery store in LA. I didn't have to attend dinner parties, engagement parties, housewarming parties and showers, baby or otherwise. Furthermore, I didn't have to think about what conclusions would be drawn from my non-attendance.

I had the mother of all excuses.

Cancer was something that happened to old people, to other people, but not to me. I was young, healthy and, I thought, well on my way to saving the universe, one Balkan country at a time. In my world, Cancer was a zodiac sign and I was untouchable. It's funny how you always think you're untouchable until you aren't. When could it have been that I got sick? What day was it? What month was it that I wasn't sick and then got sick? I turned back time in my head trying to remember when I felt the lump. When, before that, was I sure there was nothing there? Could I have done something then to save myself this ordeal? What did I do? What did I not do? What if I'd felt it sooner? Why didn't I feel it sooner? I tortured myself with these questions and finally, after months of soul-searching, none of it particularly voluntary, realised that it been my destiny.

In Bosnia they have a saying, oft repeated to me by my Man-Boy's grandmother. *Baka*, as I affectionately called her, poured me strong Turkish coffee at Sunday dinners in her tiny apartment and taught me the fundamental principle of Balkan existence:

Od sudbine nemožes pobjeći. You can't escape your destiny.

I loved Baka. I'd lost my own grandmother in adulthood, a fact that made her death all the more devastating since I'd had 26 years to forge a relationship with her. She was my rock and my biggest fan. I am convinced that had it not been for her, my parent's divorce, which I faced as an only child at the angst-ridden age of 13, would have altered my fate. As it was, though, she ensured that my life remained stable, giving me the odd moment of satire at my parents' expense. "They're crazy," she would console me when my parents were pitted against each other in dramas worthy of the Greek stage. "Don't listen to them." And I didn't, taking refuge behind her skirts and her spirit. She would cook *khoresteh bademjoon*, my favourite Persian dish, our cuisine's homage to the eggplant, and pick me up at the train station in her big blue Chevrolet. She died after my parents' divorce.

The Street of Good Fortune

When I met Baka for the first time, she was nothing like my grandmother. Tall and slender with cropped silver-white curls, she wore her good blue dress and, my Man-Boy informed me, was worried that I might be a *bula,* the colloquial term for Muslim women who veiled themselves. Man-Boy had told her his new love interest was from Iran and Baka, Serbian Orthodox from Ozren, was sure that he'd chosen a hard-core religious *Muslimanka* since he himself leaned in that direction. The first time I met her I could tell she was relieved to see my long hair flowing down the very open back of my see-through Benetton t-shirt. We instantly clicked, Baka and me. Baka's only daughter, my Man-Boy's mother, had died of cervical cancer at 34 leaving behind three children, the youngest my Man-Boy, the eldest his sister Seka. She also left behind, by all accounts, a violently abusive husband who promptly hanged himself from a tree behind their house after his wife's funeral, a scene Seka desperately tried to hide from her younger brothers before help arrived. My Man-Boy and his siblings were left in the city orphanage only to be separated when, right before the outbreak of war, Seka was sent to another institution behind what became enemy lines.

Sudbina, Destiny. Baka shook her head. "*Meri, sine, od sudbine nemožes pobjeći.*" Meri, my child, you, can't escape your destiny.

I nodded. Destiny was a fairy-tale concept to me. It was hard for me to relate to a destiny that had gone so wrong. I was raised on Disney and the Princess Bride. Destiny was the force that helped you find your Prince Charming or at least turned him into one later if he started out as a Beast.

Destiny was supposed to have a happy ending. Now it seemed it did.

For everybody else.

I spent the four months of my Summer of Chemo at home on Facebook, avoiding the sun and the heat. My official reason was that this was my only lifeline to much of the world I'd left behind, but really I became a masochistic spectator to Facebook's chronicles of my peers and "friends", whose lives had gone from strength to strength while I'd been going bald and spending the sunny days of Toronto's blink-of-an-eye summer being pumped up with toxic substances I couldn't pronounce. I knew this because of the engagement pictures, vacation pictures, party pictures and wedding albums of people I barely spoke to and hadn't thought about during my entire Bosnian existence. Lives presented to me on their Facebook profiles that proved to me that I had been wronged. I, who had no pictures of me laughing in glittering European weddings, no pictures *à deux* with a man who'd proposed, no pictures on beaches smiling and posing in colour-coordinated bikinis with equally stylish friends. No pictures at my thinnest, in my cutest outfits taken specifically for Facebook. My pictures were left behind in the Sarajevo apartment that my friend Lejla was packing up, the apartment to which I would not be returning, with all of my belongings that were now to be stored in suspended reality — like the rest of my life.

The Street of Good Fortune

This will make you a stronger person: you will see. Let me tell you how many times I was told this. For the longest time I wanted to slap anyone who gave me this line. Believe me, when you are lying on a couch — especially our couch which was wicker and about a foot shorter than me — bald, no eyebrows or eyelashes and so bloated that PMS is a fond memory, you do not feel that you are going to someday be a stronger person because this happened to you. You just don't. I don't care what anybody says. You just feel like crap. You want to know why this happened to you. You want to know what you did so terribly wrong that you got paid back in this way. You want to know why, out of all your friends and colleagues with similar upbringings and educations, out of all your peers, this happened to you. You want to know: why me? And you want to know why this hadn't happened to someone who ate exclusively junk food, was full of toxins and smoked two packs a day since high school and had been on the pill just as long (the pill, once prescribed like gummy bears to 14-year-olds who had decided to have sex or clear up a pimple, was linked to breast cancer. The first question every doctor asked me during my breast cancer world tour was, "Have you ever been on the pill?").

Your mind needs to understand why this happened to its body and, at least for me, there was no clear answer. It never ever occurred to me that I would be diagnosed with breast cancer at 34. No family history, not a smoker, not a drinker, no serious illnesses, no clues. Not one.

I had perfect breasts. A completely symmetrical, perky set of 36Bs.

I considered them my best asset and dressed them up and down, depending on the occasion. In Sarajevo, they were at the height of their career, dressed in slinky tops, coats and jackets, walking through downtown Sarajevo or the Old Market, the Baščaršija. Despite the intense competition, they held their own against their Balkan rivals.

I couldn't believe it when one of them turned on me.

I didn't want anybody to know I was sick. I told my family and my closest friends to keep it to themselves. I saw it as my life's biggest failure. I came back from my six-year Balkan adventure with no money, no job, and a tumour the size of a tangerine in my left breast. Not only had I not become Christiane Amanpour, I had even failed as a trial me. It wasn't so much that my world fell apart, since that world seemed to go on turning without me, having spat me out like a malfunctioning widget. As if the universe had decided that I was doing such a bad job at being me that I was fired. Fired and humiliated while everyone else around me seemed to continue living normal, happy lives in which they realised their goals in an almost effortless glide. The non-Bosnian girls I'd known in Sarajevo, my close friends, everybody I considered my peer group, had gotten married or pregnant or moved on to better jobs and contracts that allowed them to stay in the city or move up in UN ranks. And me, the Iranian-Canadian girl with no ambitions other than to stay in Sarajevo and complete my metamorphosis into a real *Bosanka*, who presented no threat to anybody in the highly politicised ranks of UN careerists, who didn't want to take over anybody else's job or anybody else's man, who had no designs on anybody else's patch of happiness,

The Street of Good Fortune

I got punished. Punished by The C and a forced exile back to the one place I was sure I'd put behind me; Oakville, Ontario, the absurdia suburbia that I had daydreamed for years of escaping. My life had taken such a sharp turn into uncharted territory that it seemed like the years I'd spent building my Bosnian existence had only happened in my head. In my head, I was still Christiane Amanpour, with all the time in the world to locate a hot, younger intellectual, marry him in a charming Tuscan village, and bear him a son named after a Persian emperor.

All just in time to fly to Iraq for the next chapter of my singularly successful career.

Oh my head. My poor, poor head.

It hurt to bang it against the hard, ugly thoughts that wouldn't budge. But with every bang, the scenes in my head became brighter, clearer, more vibrant. The scenes of the life I'd lived. The life I'd chosen. The life I thought had forgotten me. It was all still there, the permanent record of winning the dream life behind the right choice of door. The evidence that could prove it hadn't all just happened in my head. And more than staying alive, it became my mission to recall and save every single memory of my Bosnian existence as though my life depended on it. I pressed rewind and started watching from the very beginning.

What I realised when I got there was that Bosnia was full of Christiane Amanpours. Strong, steely, wilful women, who'd dodged bullets, survived snipers and had stories — but not to tell.

Stories hidden behind lips coloured in happy, glossy reds and pinks that left marks on white Nescafé mugs of powdered coffees, Sarajevo's drink *du jour*. Stories that seemed unbelievable coming from women who could still giggle, laugh and live, dressed with an edgy confidence that eluded me, bracelets and rings jingling against café tables as they played with their lighters and tilted their heads up at waiters while ordering coffees and speaking out of turn. Stories I couldn't have imagined if I tried, bits and pieces of which flew out during conversation as happy hands adorned with pretty, shiny nails fluttered in the air, a lit cigarette always the lucky occupant of the space between long, graceful fingers. Stories that swirled in my mind like tempests of sadness on those nights when I slept alone and thought of myself in their shoes. Eyes wide open, staring at the ceiling of my bedroom, in a country I sometimes felt was my own and sometimes, as on those nights I stared out into the dark, felt was out of my league.

Deeper, darker, and so much more complex than my light, sheltered mind could comprehend. I had no idea. No idea what my friends, the same ones whom I Nescaféd with in trendy Sarajevo locales bustling with hipness, had endured, and how they made it seem like it hadn't touched them, hadn't changed them, hadn't chipped at their spirits or dampened their aura. Just thinking about that felt like a ton of bricks on my chest. Thinking of how Olja, my ultimate Sarajevo girl, the friend who, unbeknownst to me at the time, would fly over continents to hold my body up on the toilet in Sunnybrook Hospital's emergency room, had lived through the entire war in Sarajevo, separated from her mother and sisters, alone, hungry, and exposed to snipers, grenades and shells as she made her daily trek across town and waited in line for water.

Every day.

For four years.

Or how my own Seka, my Man-Boy's sister, was thrown out of the family house in the middle of the war, pregnant along with her one-year-old Ana, on the day her husband was killed at the front. Your people killed our son, her in-laws told her as they closed the door on what remained of him. Half of my Seka, the product of a mixed marriage, was suddenly enemy territory. Twenty years old, eight months pregnant, a baby in her arms and nowhere to go, she was taken in by a neighbour. And Nina, my beautiful friend with long, Botticelli ringlets and a million eyelashes that curled framing huge brown eyes, diagnosed with ovarian cancer at twenty-eight after spending her youth in a Sarajevo encircled by guns, tanks, and snipers, a Sarajevo in which she buried all the men in her family, who sent me the last text message I received on my Bosnian phone: "Whatever happens, we women are stronger than we think."

My pity party started slowly to end. Like a fog that sometimes descended on my path, enveloping me in its thickness, I swathed myself in the warmth of self-pity at different points on my journey with The C, but never long enough to lose sight of the truth. A painful truth that cut through the fog, that brought me back to reality and reminded me just how random my good fortune was.

The day that I knew that things were not going to go so well was during my second breast biopsy at Toronto's Women's College Hospital. A biopsy is when they stick a very long needle into your tumour to take a sample to test for cancer cells. It's not a particularly painful or complex procedure, but the reason for its happening at all takes enough of a psychological toll to make you wish you were getting a series of root canals or a full gynaecological examination instead of going through a relatively painless procedure that was merely being performed because it was suspected that you might have a life-threatening disease. I lay on the bed as the nurse and doctor, both women, stood over me and thought back to two months before this day when I lay on an operating table in another hospital waiting for a nurse and a doctor, again both women, to start the first biopsy I had undergone, that time at Klinički Centar. KC was Sarajevo's main hospital located on beautiful grounds in one of my favourite parts of the city called Mejtaš, a green, hilly part surrounded by upscale residential areas reserved for doctors and professors before the war. I had for a time lived there, on a tiny side street called Čekaluša Čikma in a beautiful, renovated Austro-Hungarian-style apartment with high ceilings. What I was infinitely less familiar with was the Bosnian healthcare system which, along with the rest of Sarajevo's infrastructure, had taken a heavy blow during the war and had never really recovered. "*Ne bi ja ovdje primila injekciju* (I wouldn't even let them give me a needle there)," Amra told me. Amra was my boss at the English language school I worked at when my UN contract ran out. Amra's mother had died of breast cancer 20 years earlier; Amra went for regular breast exams. I had confided in her about my breast and she told me to leave for Canada immediately. Our colleague Selma agreed: "Meri, here you have to bribe them and you still don't get proper care." I soldiered on, assuring myself that if the care was good enough for Bosnians, it would be good enough for me. I made an appointment for a biopsy at KC, performed by a highly recommended Sarajevo gynaecologist. When my friend Naghmeh and I arrived at the hospital, I walked ahead, proud of taking my next step into authentic Bosnianness by submitting to the local healthcare system. I wasn't here to make an obscene salary in a swish UN job only to finance my first house or my summer villa on the Croatian coast and run out at soon as a better post came along. I was no international careerist. I was a diehard Bosnian now and I was going to take the good with the bad.

The waiting room had a gloomy, desolate feel, the source of which I realised was the black-and-white framed pictures that adorned the walls and surrounded us, the patients waiting on green and orange plastic chairs that were bolted to the ground. They piqued my curiosity, those pictures that covered the waiting room walls, hundreds of them, which seemed to emit an energy that I felt but couldn't name. I walked over to peer more closely at them.

And realised that the energy was dread.

Each picture was a frozen moment in the life of Sarajevo during the war, taken at the very hospital whose walls they plastered. Scenes of a sea of armless, legless, or lifeless men, women and children, and the doctors and nurses that were attempting to save them, looks of horror, despair and worst of all, helplessness, painted on their faces. Each picture was a different snapshot of the same reality. Different arms, different legs, different doctors, different nurses but the same reflection of a disaster for which they had been unprepared and to which these pictures paid homage. When a tired-looking nurse in a white smock called my name, the dread I was feeling numbed my senses as I got up and walked, zombie-like, into the room. A room with antique metal beds, old military green sheets and instruments that I had never seen on *Grey's Anatomy* or even *ER* placed on a small table in preparation for my procedure. Since the nurse didn't say anything when Naghmeh and I entered the room, my friend sat down on the chair placed beside the door and I slowly undressed, leaving my shirt and bra on her lap. Naghmeh was my roommate at the time and the sight of blood made her dizzy. I donned the gown that she'd nervously held up to her nose to make sure it was clean and saw that her face was a ghostly white. But she bravely smiled as I lay on the bed and the nurse covered me with a sheet that had a hole through which my left breast, perky and round, protruded. The doctor sat beside me and told me to relax and close my eyes but before I did, I managed to catch a glimpse of the needle she was about to stick into me. It was the thickest needle I had ever seen and it was attached to a glass measuring tube that looked like an old, clumsy version of ones I could recognise. I suddenly stopped breathing and realised that I was a foreigner – a foreigner who should not be here. I should have listened to them, to all the people who told me to go back to Canada, to the Bosnian women who couldn't believe that I had chosen to stay, to be here at Sarajevo KC when they would have done anything to be anywhere else.

The Street of Good Fortune

As I lay there in Women's College Hospital, where they'd refused to let my mother into the room even though I begged them to, where I didn't even feel the biopsy needle as it entered the already bruised site on my left breast, where an orderly waited by the door to take the samples to the lab, I remembered those other patients waiting on those orange and green plastic chairs in Sarajevo and the day that I went to the airport, soon after the result from the lab came that my tests were "inconclusive", convincing me to go home. As I lay in a Toronto hospital on a beautiful, sunny May day where the look on the nurse's face during the procedure already told me the result, I looked up at the ceiling, part of which was a painted scene of a meadow full of flowers and birds set against a bright blue sky. I said a silent thank you to that sky for having been one of those patients who had been able to get on a plane and fly out of the world I'd chosen.

3

They Found My Genes On College Street

Because my cancer was triple-negative, meaning that it had no hormonal trigger, Dr. Verma simply looked at me and said, "We can't explain why this happened. Sometimes these things just happen". I totally understood this because in Bosnia I had become familiar with things just happening. Bosnians knew better than most about the phenomenon of fundamental, life-changing, apocalyptic events that could be filed as "Sometimes these things just happen". *"Jebi ga,"* they say, *"šta se može?"* Fuck it, what can you do? *"Jebi ga"* is a statement of resignation and resilience rolled into one. Because really, in the face of such events, it's useless to rail, analyse and moan. Instead, it's best to cope Balkan style: make some strong Turkish coffee and get on with it. There is a certain freedom in resignation. It allows you to put the disaster to rest and focus on what you can control: the everyday work of living.

My everyday work of Toronto living started one day when my nurse Tammy spoke to me about genetic testing. Apparently there was something called a breast cancer gene. If I had it, that would explain why I had gotten sick. The gene was more predominant in the Ashkenazy Jewish population but did not affect only them. Since I was under the age of 35 and triple-negative, meaning there was no scientific reason why this had happened to me, I qualified for free genetic testing. Did I want to go? At first I didn't. I didn't want to know because they told me that the most prudent course of action would be to have a double mastectomy if they found the gene. And if I did have the gene, where did it come from? Which ancestor had secretly harboured a gene that would one day afflict someone not yet born? I thought back to the makeup of my family. No history of breast cancer. But what genes had I inherited and how much of the person I was, cancer and all, had to do with them?

My parents were people in transition. Having left Iran during the Islamic Revolution in their early twenties, their cultural identities were somehow fluid, and took shape over the years we lived in Canada without the opportunity ever to return to Iran. The pillars of our family were my grandparents and it was their influence that passed on to me a sense of where I was from. They were the thread that joined a life in another time and place to the unfamiliar Canadian present.

My mother's father was a self-made man. Although he became financially successful, he considered himself a scholar, an intellectual and, most important, a lover of books. Our house in Tehran on *Khiabane Khoshbakhty*, the Street of

The Street of Good Fortune

Good Fortune, housed my grandfather's enviable library with titles ranging from the autobiography of Winston Churchill to precious, handwritten, unique-edition Baha'i books that were, depending on the times, slightly or extremely dangerous to possess. Dangerous because we belonged to the Baha'i Faith, a religious minority that was and continues to be bitterly persecuted in the country of its birth. My grandfather was a well-respected Baha'i member of the community. He sat on various committees, the most notable of which was the Baha'i publishing committee, where he edited manuscripts. He was happiest when he was reading and this is how I always remember him: in his grey armchair, with his thick, brown-rimmed glasses from Iran, and a book. Once we moved to Canada my grandfather's love of books and reading were his constant companions and confidants, although instead of sitting in the library of his beautiful house in Tehran, decorated with mirrors and with mouldings of angels and flowers trimming the ceilings, he read in the living room of the rented two-bedroom apartment that was his home in exile. As far as my child's eye could see, he didn't seem to mind. He never complained. With a bookcase filled with only a fraction of the books he had painstakingly acquired during his lifetime, the only books that could be taken out of Iran at a moment's notice during those early days of revolution, he maintained a serene sense of dignity and continuity that belied his roots.

He was born in 1919 in Hamadan's Jewish ghetto. Hamadan is a town 160 miles southwest of Tehran and has since biblical times been home to a Jewish community. He lost his mother at the age of four, a blow from which he never recovered, leaving him with a certain aura of sadness that was part of his character and could be felt by those around him. Soon after, my great-grandfather and a surprisingly substantial number of his fellow Hamadani Jews, along with tens of thousands of Iranians, converted to the Baha'i Faith, a religion whose followers were even more persecuted than Jews. This is how my grandfather met and married my grandmother, a *Siyyid,* a member of a family who could allegedly trace their ancestry back to the Prophet Muhammad. An unlikely pairing, to say the least, but, in retrospect, genetically desirable.

Could it have been their genes that sealed my fate?

My father's father was a Kurd. Of the minority ethnic groups in Iran, the Kurds represent about seven per cent of the Iranian population. He was a large, happy man with big, kind hands and a wonderful smile. The only picture I have of him is still in Sarajevo with the rest of my belongings but the look on his face in that picture is how I remember him, content and unassuming. He was quiet and gentle and, as a child, I just liked being around him. Like my mother's father, he had lost his mother as a small boy and soon afterwards made his way to Tehran looking for work. While he never became a rich man, what makes him stand out for me is that he fell in love with and married my grandmother, a divorcée with a child. In Iran at the time, and even now, this is extremely unusual, to say the least. Regular men seek out virgins that are, as we say in Farsi, "*aftab mahtab nadideh*", unexposed to sunlight or moonlight, or, in a word, "untouched". The fact that a man with a future would choose to marry a "used" woman reflected a heroic disregard for convention that I can only hope to have inherited, even if it did come along with a cancer gene. Things were complicated by the fact that my grandfather was, by his own admission, a Suni Muslim, while my grandmother's family, staunchly against this match, was Shiite. The truth, revealed to my mother years later in Canada right before my grandfather was about to undergo anaesthesia for a hernia operation, was that he had actually been born a Jew. Apparently one per cent of Iran's Kurds are Jews. My grandfather's father had converted his family to Suni Islam after fleeing an anti-Semitic pogrom in his own village. For my grandfather's sister, this conversion was too much. Another in a battery of losses she had already endured, she committed suicide, throwing herself from the rooftop of their house.

And so it came to be that, sitting at my genetic testing appointment in the College Street offices of the renowned Dr. Narod, the geneticist and discoverer of the breast cancer gene, I was unable to fill in medical histories for the Jewish women in my family, not one of whom had survived long enough for there to be a record of how she had lived. I peered down at the family tree I had been given where, with my father's help, I filled in the names of the women in his family and wrote my own name in the blank last space at the bottom of the page. A lonely circle with my name, date of birth, and *"locally advanced breast cancer in l. breast, triple negative, diagnosed 2007"* stared back at me. What looked like a kindergarten lesson depicting shapes connected to each other by lines suddenly turned into a picture that spoke a thousand words.

Words I wished I could forget.

Dr. Narod was a national hero/mad scientist. We were very lucky to get an appointment. My father and I sat in his reception area where we were met by his assistant Aletta, who was extremely pleasant and explained how the genetic testing procedure would work. Then she was joined by Dr. Narod, who sat down and peered at the laptop my father had brought with the images of all of my various scans. When he began to speak, I knew for sure he was a genius. He spoke English, but it might as well have been Sanskrit. I braced myself and tried again to understand what he was saying.

English. Check.

Words. Check.

Sentences. Not so much.

I looked at my father and realised that he was having the same problem. Thankfully though, Aletta seemed to understand the language of genius and translated for us. She explained that she would take my blood and then call me to discuss the results. I shouldn't be worried that I would be called in, she explained, because they called everyone in no matter what the results showed. She said, though, that a positive result for the breast cancer gene would mean some serious choices to make. I blocked out the statistics that she started to rattle off about the chances of the cancer returning both in my breasts and also in my ovaries to process at a later time when I could free more room in my brain for life and death matters. Then my father and I went across the street to Fran's Diner and celebrated crossing one more hurdle in this surreal journey with an unclear destination.

My father and I had, following my flight to the "Bolsheviks", the term my father used to describe any culture east of Vienna, a strained relationship. He couldn't understand why the only child he'd whisked out of revolution and schooled in Canada's best educational institutions had decided to escape behind the defunct Iron Curtain instead of taking up his offer of an apartment downtown and a life of achievement. "Can't you just stay in Canada for a year and see how it goes?" he begged me as I packed my belongings the day after the Call to the Bar, the ceremony that admitted me to the legal profession, one of his proudest moments.

I couldn't.

Really and truly I couldn't wait to get out. I'd planned my escape from the monotony of normality for so long that the idea of staying in it for even one more minute was not an option. In my head I was already off.

Off to become Christiane Amanpour on my personal Balkan Express.

My father came to visit me in Sarajevo. He was horrified. To be fair, his trip had begun badly. The pilot had not been able to land at Sarajevo's airport and, while people prayed, with hands up to their faces, reciting the *Fatiha*, the opening verses of the Quran, pulled the plane up just in time not to crash into a mountain wall. When I arrived to pick him up, it was an aged version of the man I'd seen the summer before that walked into the arrivals hall. As if that trauma wasn't enough, having watched his own country sink in the mediaeval quicksand of an Islamic Revolution, he did not look fondly upon the mosques and veiled women he encountered at every corner in post-war Sarajevo. The fact that the veils were sexy, sequinned pieces of tulle in shiny pinks, blues and purples covering the heads of heavily made-up Balkan Barbies pursing glossy lips as they sashayed down the street, did not console him. "There will be revolution here," he declared ominously. "They will take over here too, just wait and see." I tried to explain to him that many of these girls were wearing miniskirts until yesterday and that many would return from their Scheherezade-inspired fashion phase sooner or later but it drew a look of disdain. Disdain that I was dumb enough to believe that it took more than a superficial layer of religious identification to allow a political mafia to usurp power.

What he and I agreed on, and always had, was on café time. I am the ultimate café girl. Don't make me live anywhere where there is no café and Tim Horton's doesn't count. Sarajevo, home to a café for every square metre of land, was my natural habitat. This proclivity I had inherited from my dad. He and I could sit for hours at cafés and simply be. The only happy times of my father's Bolshevik-bound voyage were our sittings at the many cafés we visited. During that week, we saw the inside of every single café at least once. I took him to the Old Market, to those small, smoke-filled, Ottoman style coffeehouses where an old woman would bring us Turkish coffees in traditional Bosnian *džezvas*, tiny copper receptacles on a little round tray accompanied by a sugar dusted, pink square of Turkish delight. "*Oh, Babo ti je došao!*" the owners would exclaim, your dad is visiting! They were always grateful when someone who didn't have to, and wasn't getting paid to, visited their country of ill-repute. *Babo* was the colloquial term for Dad, similar to *Baba* in Farsi and woven into Serbo-Croatian from the time of Ottoman rule. It was one of the many words we also used in Farsi that peppered the language spoken in my new home.

"*Da, da,*" I would respond. Yes, yes. "*Kako mu se svidja Sarajevo?*" Does he like Sarajevo? How could I explain that Sarajevo never had a chance with Babo? That the city represented to him a void into which his only child had fallen and out of which even the promise of Toronto real estate couldn't tempt her. He spent the entire trip attempting to extricate me from the clutches of this cursed place that had, for no reason he could decipher, swallowed me. Even more passionately, he attempted to save me from an ill-fated relationship with a young, confused *mujahedeen* sympathiser, the thought of whom made my parents forget their years of pre- and post-divorce strife and rally with united resolve to undo this match. Man-Boy hadn't been to university, was a self-professed *mujahedeen*, and had a job at a Persian carpet gallery, courtesy of yours truly. I knew enough not to introduce him to my father. Man-Boy insisted, firmly believing that, despite a calamitous meeting with my mother who'd visited the summer before, a man-to-man talk with my father, in which he was confident in his ability to bond with his own kind, would turn the tides in favour of our relationship. My protests fell on deaf ears and one day under extreme duress I took Man-Boy to lunch with my father at Michele, one of Sarajevo's busiest restaurants. My father barely looked in his direction and made no attempts to veil his disapproval, mostly appearing flabbergasted to be sitting in his company. "Your father is a snob," I was told at home when, overwhelmed with the stress of my father's trip and Man-Boy's incessant wounded whining, I collapsed on the couch in my flat.

My father returned home to Toronto having failed to bring me back with him. I emerged from his trip even more determined to remain in my city at any cost, *iz inata* as they would say in Bosnia. Further translation: Out of an obstinate determination to prove him wrong. To prove everybody wrong and make my Become Christiane Amanpour adventure a resounding success. The game was on in the battle of wills between my father and me and the chilly relations between us continued until… Until the night I returned from the fertility clinic with an enemy breast and a sudden, jarring exposure to the world of anonymous sperm. Having weathered this initial storm on her own, my mother had called Babo to come to the house. Thus began a new relationship between my father and me in which he took it squarely upon himself to save my life. If there had been any gaps in his record of fatherhood, any doubts as to his presence in my life or upbringing, his singular, laser-like focus on my person during my darkest hour made up for it.

My father is the most gifted, hard-working person I know. *Nije što je moj*, not because he's mine but because it's true. Frankly, it wasn't something that I felt really worked in my favour until only recently. He finished every task he started completely and to perfection and expected the same from his progeny.

That would be me.

While he was a mathematical wizard and a talented architect, math pained me and I could never draw past a remedial kindergarten level. One day when I was an 11-year-old budding ballerina more resembling a baby duck than any kind of swan, I was practising pirouettes in the family room. He watched me as I repeatedly attempted to turn 360 degrees on half tiptoe with my right foot placed under my left knee, always falling out at 280. In his dress pants and socks he said, "Look, you have to understand the physics of it," and pirouetted perfectly, touching down at the end of the turn, light as a feather. "See?" I saw all right. I saw that I would never be good enough. When I was accepted to law school, my father was overjoyed. Finally, I would amount to something. He funded my summer study trips to Oxford and The Hague with the long-term hope that I would end up in the corner office of a well-known Toronto law firm having, through some epiphany, cultivated a robust respect for real estate and RRSPs that could only stem from either the insecurity that loss of home and country can bring, or long exposure and residence in a world of establishment, entitlement and stability. I had experienced neither.

When I did occupy the corner room in really what was the penthouse of one of the best-known buildings on Toronto's patch of real estate heaven, our very own version of the Champs Elysées, University Avenue, it wasn't exactly what either of us had had in mind during those dreamy days of law school reverie. Despite its enviable location, nobody ever wanted to occupy any kind of a room, penthouse or otherwise, in Princess Margaret Hospital. The silver lining to this unexpected cloud in my breast was that it brought my parents and me together as a family, if only briefly. My father spent every day at our house and drove me to biweekly chemo sessions where he'd run to the hospital's food court to satisfy my sudden cravings for cream cheese bagels and pasta as the chemo cocktail made its way into my bloodstream. He was there to share my sudden appreciation for third-rate modern Iranian cinema, which he downloaded on his laptop and watched with me every night on my mother's white wicker couch. He ate dinner with us, or at least the first round of dinner since I was constantly ravenously hungry and "dinner" was a term used for the several meals I ate after six pm. It was the first time I remember eating dinner together as a family.

I was never one of those children who'd dreamt of having her parents get back together. When I was 13 years old my mother separated from her childhood sweetheart and the man with whom she'd had a turbulent 17-year marriage. One day she sat with me at the kitchen table in the matrimonial home in east Oakville and told me that she would return to him if I wanted her to. I told her that she shouldn't turn back on my account and from then on we became a family of women: me, my mother and my grandmother, who later came to live with us in my mother's post-divorce townhouse in a happy little crescent.

We are not women of the home. It is not the arena in which we excel. We don't bake cookies or banana loaf and we don't have recipe books or expensive cooking knives jutting out of wooden blocks in our kitchens. We don't recognise the difference between granite countertops and whatever was there before and we don't feel safe spending time at sinks where pots and pans hang from above.

It's genetic.

My grandmother was one of Tehran's rare female drivers in the 1950s. Because her husband was epileptic, she was the only person in the family who drove, a skill she carried over to Canada, taking me to ballet lessons and picking me up from school. I was not thrilled when my mother put her in charge of transportation. My mother was notoriously late in picking me up, but my grandmother was always on time and often early, which meant that she would park the car, march into the ballet school full of long-legged girls in pink tights and blonde buns stretching before class, and yell out my name into the tiny building. Mortified, I would attempt to control the upward movement of my plié and the corresponding arm position as my name was bellowed across the tinkling of the piano. Despite the untold number of embarrassing incidents that ensued when my grandmother arrived early, to school, to ballet, or in front of the train station to pick me up, I always knew that she was an extraordinary woman. Not just because we adored each other and fought over the remote control, me vying for *Oprah* while she was on team *The Price is Right*. Not because I was her official interpreter for *The Young and the Restless*, our favourite soap opera, a post I held from the age of 12, during which I learned to translate scandalous phrases like "Nikki, I want to make love to you" into Farsi's *"Mesle eenke mikhad ba Nikki karhaye bad bokone,"* giggling with delight as she and I exchanged knowing looks under the disapproving eye of my mother. Not for any of those reasons, but because she taught me to be myself, to be fearless, and to love without restraint.

In a world of Persian women obsessed with an image that required a large collection of jewellery snatched from the jaws of revolution and worn defensively, pre-Facebook, to persuade each other of happiness and success, my grandmother kept it real. She was uninterested in any form of display and had no desire to amass trinkets or become trapped in an image of pre-revolutionary wealth. She was, however, determined to learn English upon her arrival in her "prison" country, as she referred to Canada when the temperature dipped to below human. Every day, she'd pack up her girls, her two Iranian friends that lived in our building and drive to English as a Second Language classes where she would struggle with the letters of a language she'd been introduced to at 60 with the curiosity and persistence of a young girl that had her whole life ahead of her.

"*Dorost neveshtam?*" Did I spell it correctly? she would ask me, showing me the piece of paper where she'd written a column of English words in awkward Latin letters with a translation in Farsi script beside it. After her death we found these pieces of paper all over the house, proving that my grandmother studied as though she would live forever. And I was sure she would. Her death, outside of being the biggest loss I'd ever endured, was also the biggest shock I'd ever known. In my mind, she was invincible. She reminded me every day that she wasn't going anywhere. Sometimes I'd watch her sleep as I walked by her room and find myself checking to make sure she was breathing. Since she, like my mother and me, slept with the blankets covering her head, it took me a good 10 to 15 seconds to verify that the blanket moved slightly with the rhythm of her breath. The second before I would begin to panic she'd throw back the cover, eyes still closed, teeth still on nightstand, and announce, *"Hanooz zendam naneh — negaran nabash, man nemimiram"*. I'm still alive my child, don't worry, I'm not going to die.

My grandmother, like all women before her, and many after her, had not chosen her fate. Wife and mother were roles imposed upon her by culture and circumstance but within their confines, her fighting spirit and wilful personality, as well as her incredible luck in being married to a kind, patient and solvent man, allowed her a life in which she was able to be herself. This was a fact she celebrated, recognising its value and staunchly refusing to conform to norms she didn't accept.

"Did he kiss you?" she would ask with a mischievous smile whenever I would come home from a date.

"MADAR!!" my mother would protest, "Don't teach her these things!"

My grandmother, well aware that, at 25, I had already been taught these things, continued. "Do you love him?" she would ask.

"Only marry him if you love him." My mother had been the first in the family to follow my grandmother's advice, marrying her math tutor at 17, a match staunchly opposed by her parents, who considered my mother far too young and my father far too Shiite despite his recent conversion to the Baha'i Faith. After my mother's short hunger strike and the discovery of letters penned by my lovesick father threatening to ingest rat poison if she was kept from him, my parents were married in a beautiful ceremony at Tehran University's *Bashgah*, banquet hall. Four years later I was born, the first grandchild in both my parents' families.

My first memory of Iran is of my mother and me and watermelons. We were on summer vacation at the Caspian coast, Shomal, as it's known, and I was walking with my mother after lunch, which included watermelon for dessert, in a hotel that catered to vacationers up from Tehran. We left by the rear entrance of the hotel where a dirt road led up to a forest. I heard a man yelling, chastising somebody, and then my mother turned around, surveyed the scene, and yelled back, "Leave them alone. They're not hurting anybody". I saw that the yeller was a hotel employee barking at a dirty, dishevelled woman with her children around her, eating watermelon rinds from the garbage dump behind the hotel. I was five years old, the first time I realised that not everybody lived like I did. Exposure to poverty for a five-year-old Iranian child in 1978 was probably not uncommon. Revolution was brewing and the avant-garde children's literature of the time included books like the one my father had bought for me, which chronicled a little girl's visit to her nanny's house. In our house we also had a nanny who often came to work with her own little girl, my playmate, and I thought of her whenever my father read this book to me. A book beautifully illustrated with heart-wrenching paintings of the nanny's living conditions compared to the beautiful house she cleaned and the little girl dressed in a pretty pink frock standing beside the nanny's children, who were dressed in rags and too poor to be able to afford schoolbooks. Part of the story involved one of the nanny's children getting sick: the family could not afford to pay for a doctor. But it was only on the day of the watermelons that I understood that the poverty I saw around me resulted directly from the unfairness inherent in my world, which had favoured me at the expense of the woman and her children eating rinds of the watermelon that had just been served to me, quite literally, on a silver platter. My good fortune wasn't random. It had been gained at her expense. And on that day I felt a sense of guilt mixed, as I grew up, with a sense of responsibility to somewhat change that scene in my pre-revolutionary country where my family and I would soon be in danger.

I also remember years, or what seemed like years in child-memory time, of the phone ringing in our Oakville apartment and my mother freezing with fear before answering. In those years of revolution, and afterwards, our little apartment got calls from friends and family in Iran informing my mother of friends, colleagues and professors killed or kidnapped for being Baha'is. My first childhood memories of Canada are of my mother sitting on her silk wedding carpet, on top of the blue and red peacocks that adorned each corner, tears rolling down her face as she held the phone to her ear. I would tense up as soon as I heard the phone ring and could tell as soon as she answered whether this would be one of those calls. When my mother was 26 and I was five, she returned to Iran to sell my grandfather's property and bring back whatever she could save. She spent three months in a power flux that oscillated between lawlessness, fear, and a tiny sliver of hope. When she left her homeland for the last time after selling, for a tiny fraction of its worth, everything my grandfather had built from the age of nine, when he'd come to Tehran to work, until the age of 65 when he was forced into exile, neither she nor the country she pined for would ever be the same.

For Iranians, time was divided into before and after the revolution. In Sarajevo, time was divided between before and after the war. Both were defining moments in history where everything that was known crumbled and a new reality arose; that perhaps preventable slice of time, an invisible border cutting through lives, relationships, and emotions against which life before and after was measured. In my world, time was divided by cancer. In my post-cancer mind, my pre-cancer life was a happy place where I was in control of my destiny and happiness. A place with which I could find no fault except for the inescapable fact that it was a place that led me to that slice of time, that moment in which my breast became my enemy, in which all the events that had led to that moment became suspects for somehow triggering a dip in my immune system which couldn't defend itself against a mutation that caused my downfall. My language reflected as much. Most of my sentences began, "When I was sick…", "Before I got sick…", and "During chemo…". The defining moment in my personal history became cancer, this sinister force that had popped up out of nowhere, for no apparent reason, to destroy my well-intentioned life.

4

A Tree Grows in Oakville Except It's Not an Oak

When we came to Canada I spoke no English and had a weird name. Despite the fact that Maryam is, according to one of the original languages of the Bible, the actual name of Mary Magdalene and the mother of Christ, I spent much of my childhood sounding it out for various teachers, ballet instructors and friends' parents as they scowled in confusion with the phonetics of Maryam which compared to the Jennifers, Heathers and Michelles in my class was a challenging arrangement of letters.

When I arrived in Bosnia, no one scowled when I told them my name. I was instantly welcomed by *"OH Merima! Meryema! Ti si Meri, Naša Meri"*. You are Meri, our Meri. Bosnians, as it turned out, had many of the same names I grew up with. I was Merima, Meri for short, and there were

Minas, Lejlas, Aidas, Mirzas, Oljas and Anitas. It was the first thing that struck me: they had our names. Or we had their names. I didn't care but I suddenly felt a click inside my soul like when the seat in the car finally settles in to its proper position while you are driving and you feel a sense of relief mingled with comfort. It was that feeling of relief mingled with comfort that followed me on my Bosnian odyssey, relief that here was a place where I captured that feeling of home, a feeling that had gone missing for me since my childhood exile. And I let go of my past, my ideas, opinions and attitudes formed over 24 years of life in exile, allowing myself to be enveloped in the warmth of that feeling as it led me into the cities, the bus-rides, the flats, the taxis, the living-rooms, the municipal offices, the refugee camps, the Nissan land cruisers, the orphanages, and the little red Volkswagen hatchback that filled up my daily existence in my new home.

Some people find themselves in faraway ashrams under the tutelage of gurus suddenly discovering the meaning of life while meditating in Downward Dog. Some people find themselves walking through Spain, trekking a path from one mediaeval church to another in search of epiphany. Others find themselves in retreat, a hermit-like existence in some rural cabin, hoping to destroy their demons.

I found myself when I lost myself. And I did lose myself. I lost myself voluntarily, leaping into this familiar unknown with an eager running start. I lost myself, happily drowning in a sea of otherness with no desire to ever come up for air. I lost myself in the hills and valleys, the villages, the music, the love, the hate, the blood and the irony that can only be found in Bosnia.

The Street of Good Fortune

I lost myself and they found me.

They found me in the tiny, hilly, cobblestone alleys of Sarajevo's Old Town that I walked every day on my way to drink coffee in the men-only *birtija,* coffeehouse, on Kovači hill overlooking *Sebilj,* Sarajevo's Pigeon Square, home to an Ottoman-style fountain flanked by coffeehouses and one of Sarajevo's oldest mosques, a domed structure surrounded by an overgrown patch of green bushes that welcomed the faithful with a carefully tended rose garden at its gate, happy red and yellow roses peeking out from the iron railings. They found me in Bentbaša, the subject of the most beautiful Bosnian folk songs, the breathtaking mountain trail above the Miljačka River that divided Sarajevo and was the reason for a series of bridges, built in different styles, I wanted to believe, by rebel architects refusing to submit to conventional aesthetic norms. On Sundays I would walk the length of Bentbaša, stopping first for coffee at the wooden terrace of the Bazeni restaurant at the entrance to the trail, shaded from the sun by the trees around it before walking along the river, silently admiring the majesty of the craggy mountain face that loomed before me. They found me in Vilsonovo Šetalište, the pedestrian alley named after Woodrow Wilson, lined on both sides by great chestnut trees that cast a particular shade of dusk upon the city's young lovers who kissed incognito on park benches strategically placed under them. They found me waiting on the steps of the Cathedral, the unofficial centre of the city, the meeting point where Sarajevo's nights on the town began. "*Vidimo se kod Katedrale (*Let's meet at the Cathedral)," was the standard confirmation for any Sarajevo date. They found me in the great Post Office, the renovated

Austro-Hungarian edifice where I would wait, guarding my precious place in line with an angry glare and on-guard elbows, a skill honed over months of practice, to pay my bills, buy my phone cards, and pick up packages. They found me in the tiny café facing Muzička škola, Sarajevo's music school, where I would order coffee that easily passed for turpentine just so I could listen while invisible fingers flawlessly delivered wild Beethoven Sonatas and tamed Rachmaninov's impossible piano concertos.

The only child of an Iranian immigrant family, unconventional by birth, catapulted by revolution and persecution into the cold, Anglo-Saxon bastion of Oakville, Ontario, where revolution was a foreign concept and persecution a spelling- test zinger, had found a place where she felt at home. The girl who clearly remembered landing in a frozen Toronto November and wondering why in the world her parents had brought her there, who used to ask her mother every night when they would be going back home to her grandparents, who still to this day feels a wave of sadness when she drives by the Glengrove Suites, her first Toronto apartment of that cold November exile, had returned Home to a foreign country.

My mother insisted on private schools and ballet lessons. She wanted me to get the best education possible, ensuring that, despite the fact that we were in a new country, we maintained the same standards of cultural and educational life that we'd had in Iran. St. Mildred's, an Anglican ladies' college, and the stuffy ballet schools I attended for years, did not at the time house a significant immigrant population. I remembered the first time I attended "chapel", the obligatory morning ritual at St. Mildred's, which included the Lord's Prayer and hymn singing. I wasn't Anglican but, growing up as a Baha'i child, I was taught to believe in Christ, knew prayers in English, Farsi and Arabic by heart and, most important, had been instilled with a deep sense of reverence for religion, which included silence during prayer. As we all sat in lines according to our grades in the school's gym, and then stood up to pray, girls around me giggled and rolled their eyes as prayers began, dropping their red hymn books engraved with golden crosses on the pile of textbooks topped with Roots pencil cases at their feet.

I froze in shock.

I waited for a teacher to give them The Look. The same look my mother gave me if I so much as twitched during prayers, a look that pierced through space and time and caused the unfortunately situated friends that sat next me to fall silent and squeak "Your mother is looking at us" if I failed to notice.

Nothing happened.

Instead I was shot a menacing look by the homeroom teacher for looking around. She was a mean-spirited PhD whose dissatisfaction at ending up as an overqualified high-school teacher was visible and, for reasons I could not understand, would don what I only later identified as a Henry the Eighth costume for the more ceremonial religious events of the school calendar.

Suffice it to say that I was a misfit in my new world of WASP. My Oscar-winning emotional range, stifled by assimilation to an environment where the temperature hovered between numb and more numb, to a school where I was not like the others, it was no wonder that I wholly identified with a country where emotion trumped reason and where tomorrow was never more important than right now. And despite my awkwardness in my surroundings, I didn't feel Iranian. I didn't pine for a country I could barely remember so much as I pined for a feeling that I belonged. I was the best student in my English class in spite of its being taught by the overqualified PhD whose note in my Grade 11 report card, "Maryam must learn to persuade by facts rather than emotion," I looked back upon with a certain sense of smug triumph. This didn't deter me from my avid and, might I add, deeply emotional love of reading and writing. I think, like all immigrant children, I understood the culture I lived in as an outside observer who had another culture with which to compare it, even though I never returned to Iran. I was forced to endure Saturday morning Farsi classes which taught me to be semi-literate in a language in which persuasion relies strictly upon the use of emotion and yet managed to produce the likes of Rumi and Omar Khayyam.

High school is just so overrated.

"*Jesi li udata?*" Are you married?

In the almost six years that I lived in Sarajevo, I never sat in a taxi where the driver did not pose this question right after I, with my obvious foreign accent that I so wanted to believe didn't exist, directed them where to take me. It's not that they thought I was a foreigner. No, the consolation for having been reminded of my lack of fluency in a language I prided myself on mastering was that they actually thought I was one of them. But part of the Diaspora. And therefore possessed a valuable passport.

In the Diaspora were the many thousands who had left Bosnia to live in the West, either as refugees during the war or as immigrants before it. The Diaspora descended upon Sarajevo every summer, reminding the locals that they still lived in a post-war country where jobs were scarce, opportunities minimal, and pensions virtually non-existent. Diaspora season was hook-up season in Sarajevo, where single Diasporans came looking for suitable spouses to take back with them and local singles made themselves available, happy to fall in love with the opportunity to leave. Following the war, Bosnia had a strict visa regime, meaning that unless you wanted to travel to Turkey or Malaysia you needed a visa which, for most Bosnians, was extremely difficult to get. As I walked to work every morning I would pass the long, long lines that formed, rain or shine, in front of the German, French and Austrian embassies, all occupying some of Sarajevo's most beautiful villas in the same chic quarter of the city. Lines of Bosnians waiting to see if they would be granted permission to enter the hallowed grounds of the countries whose citizens lived luxurious, tax-free lifestyles in Sarajevo while working for the innumerable international organisations that offered six- figure, tax-free, euro salaries to their "international" — code for non-Bosnian — employees.

"*Nisam* (not married)," I'd sigh as I looked out the window, all too familiar with the taxi-driver routine. Then the fun would really start. *"ZAŠTO?"* Why not? *"STA FALI NAMA SARAJLIJAMA?"* What's wrong with us Sarajevo boys? They would bellow, highly indignant. No offence to Sarajevo taxi drivers, all of whom engaged me in many an existential conversation and to whom I am indebted for much of my language instruction, but generally speaking they were rather large, imposing, chain smokers in their early fifties with a level of self-confidence I wished I could bottle.

Once I made the mistake of telling one of them that I did have a boyfriend, but that he was from Zenica, a city 70 km away from Sarajevo, home to an under-functioning steel factory and Čelik, the soccer team that were arch-rivals of Sarajevo's. My driver slammed on the brakes. I looked around to see what he'd stopped to avoid only to hear him yell; *"IZ ZENICE?"* FROM ZENICA? *"Toliko Sarajlija ovdje i ti nadje Zeničanina?"* So many good Sarajevo boys and you get conned by a guy from Zenica?

Years later, back in Canada and eating through more than my fair share of the healthcare system, I thought of that taxi driver. I wondered if I had indeed been conned by a guy from Zenica. I wondered if things would have been different if I'd ended up with a Sarajevo boy. Would he have been by my side during chemo sessions, holding my hand as I drifted off to sleep from the Reactine that Dr. Verma prescribed to avoid the choking reaction I got from the chemo cocktail? Would he have told me it didn't matter when my hair fell out, followed by my eyelashes and then my eyebrows, that he still loved me no matter what? Would he have sat next to me, patiently watching me hour after hour, day after day, while I lay on my mother's white wicker couch, bloated, depressed and resembling an extraterrestrial? Would he have taken the risk that I might not make it and stood by me anyway?

I would never know.

Which, in the end, was probably a good thing.

Sarajevo girls, though, now they were a different story. Sarajevo girls you never had to wonder about. Sarajevo girls you could count on. Sarajevo girls came through when it mattered most.

"Almira is coming to visit you," Olja shouted across the bad phone connection when I was back in Toronto.

"What?"

I could barely hear what she was shouting away off on the Ivory Coast. Olja was one of my Sarajevo girls. We'd worked together at the UNHCR (the United Nations High Commissioner for Refugees). She was my personal guide to the city: she knew everybody and everybody knew her. We ate lunch together every day at Buon Gusto, a little Italian restaurant behind the burned out Presidency building and across the street from our offices at the UNITIC Towers, the twin skyscrapers of the United Investment and Trading Company, shelled during the war. Buon Gusto was owned by Emir, a staple *gradska faca*, city face, a person born in Sarajevo, and a familiar face about town. Since Olja was also a *gradska faca*, by association I was able to benefit from a depth of social and cultural experience elusive to most foreigners. Olja took me to my first Bosnian play at the National Theatre; her connections with the annual Sarajevo Film Festival always got us tickets to the most coveted movies. She introduced me to singers and film producers, people I recognised from the media, when they stopped to greet her in the street. "He went to grade school with me," she informed me when a famous Sarajevo director walked by. "Now he thinks he's too good to say hello." She made a face. My all-time favourite Olja moment took place in a taxi at the taxi-stand at Strossmeyer in front of Hotel Evropa, the half-destroyed one-time five-star hotel of Yugoslavia's most eclectic capital. This taxi line-up was famous for the hardball attitudes of its drivers. In true anti-capitalist fashion, they loitered around their cars, smoking, joking and complaining that they made no money while refusing any fare for distances they considered too short, a very subjective calculation. I had, long before, stopped using that taxi-stand, choosing instead to walk or to hail empty taxis driving down the street, a cardinal sin if done in sight of the drivers waiting in line. I developed great legs walking up and down even the 90-degree angle Bijelave hill, fearing the wrath of the taxi drivers who never forgot a face. But this time, as we approached the notorious yellow cars, Olja was with me. If anyone could take on a Strossmeyer taxi driver, it was Olja. As we approached, Olja in front, me trailing behind, I noticed the first driver, a seven-foot giant and the well-known leader of the Stross-bullies. On hearing our destination, he stuck his face right up to her nose as she was about to get into his taxi.

The Street of Good Fortune

"I didn't fight in the war for four years so I could drive you for five marks."

She did not miss a beat. In one move, she entered the taxi, slid across the back seat to the other side; where she opened the door, stuck one foot out and her face right back into his. "And I didn't survive the war for four years to give you five marks. *Pička ti materina!*" An untranslatable expletive that involved his mother, a part of her anatomy, and Olja's desire that he should return there. The giant deflated. Following her lead, I elatedly slid across the back seat and emerged from the other side, and slammed the door. Bosnian women didn't mess around.

They were in charge. Mostly because they did everything.

The first time I took the bus from Sarajevo to the town of Zenica, I spent the entire time looking out of the bus window as we drove by the villages that connected the capital to Central Bosnia and saw women, often very old women, bent over, working the land, raking, hoeing, gardening, and feeding the chickens. My foreign girl brain kicked in. Poor women, I thought, obviously the men had been killed in the war and they were widows, forced to maintain their land alone. The next bus-ride though, I sat on the other side of the bus. The café side. It turned out that, although many men had been killed in the war, many more were now sitting in the nation's cafés, smoking with their buddies while their wives, mothers and daughters did everything.

"Almira is coming to visit you," yelled Olja again. This time I heard her. I knew Almira through Olja. They were friends from university which they'd attended during the war and Almira worked in the UNITIC building too but in the OSCE, the Organisation for Security and Co-operation in Europe, which its international staff cheerfully dubbed the Organisation for Sipping Coffee in Europe. As local staff, Almira had to punch in and out on a time card to ensure she wasn't sipping coffee with her international bosses.

Almira, who had recently married a Canadian she'd met in Sarajevo and moved to Quebec, had heard of my situation from Olja, now stationed with UNHCR in the Ivory Coast.

"She'll take the bus and she'll call you to let you know when she arrives."

After she arrived, Almira walked arm-in-arm with me through the wooded path behind my house, as she told me stories of her family. To me, she represented Sarajevo. She was half-Serb, half-Muslim, but one aunt was Croat and the other Jewish. Sarajevo had been home to a small, vibrant Jewish community since 1500, when several thousand Sephardic Jews had fled Spain and its Inquisition. Many had mixed with the locals and so some of Sarajevo's families were combinations of Muslims, Jews, Catholics and Orthodox. Several beautiful synagogues, along with mosques and churches, were the reason Sarajevo was called the Jerusalem of Europe. Almira's Jewish aunt had been saved from the occupying Nazis during the Second World War.

The Street of Good Fortune

Almira visited me three times during my Summer of Chemo, the first four months of my treatment where I broke down to her in our wooded walks about how I didn't think I would make it through what seemed to be my downward spiral. I cried and railed and she listened.

"*Polako, Meri, moraš biti strpljiva.*" Easy, Meri, you need to have patience. Almira had recently lost her mother to cancer, having nursed her until the end. She was newly wed, and in a new home, so I felt badly that she had to spend so much of her time with me, in my emotional state. She saved me then with her quiet, gentle manner and her stories, her beautiful, amazing Sarajevo stories. Stories of how her grandfather, a tailor, saved his Jewish niece from Jasenovac, the Nazi death camp in Croatia, by befriending a Nazi officer whose uniform he altered. I pictured him on his knees, pins in his mouth, sweating at the feet of a Nazi officer in full regalia. I pictured him thinking what to do, what to say, knowing that the fate of his niece, the child whose parents had already perished, was in his hands and only he had this one chance to get her back. She told me stories of her parents, devout believers in Tito's Yugoslavia who celebrated both Muslim Bajram and Orthodox New Year, and their horror when the latest war tore their dream apart. She told me of how she once visited a friend's house when Sarajevo went hungry during the first winter of war, and saw that they were cooking. That winter there had been nothing to cook. This family were political bigwigs who'd never stopped cooking, and they offered her coffee, strong Turkish coffee. With sugar.

Sugar was the equivalent of gold bars during the war. She recounted that she sweetened her coffee with so much sugar that it was no longer liquid: it was the best coffee she'd ever tasted. On Almira's last visit, Olja joined us and we walked and laughed and cried. That fall, from a hospital bed in Sunnybrook, I thought of our time together and realised that, I too, had survived.

5

IT HAPPENED IN THE SHOWER

ONE DAY I was taking a shower in the bathroom of my *mahala* apartment. *Mahala* is the word for neighbourhood in Turkish, referring to the Old Town residential areas of Sarajevo, dotting the surrounding hills and dating back to Ottoman times. The cobblestone alleys, the tiny old mosques interspersed between the stone houses built with *avlijas*, courtyards, in front of them, enchanted me. I loved living there. I loved the sound of the local muezzin during the call to prayer at sunrise, giving me a feeling of security like a reminder that God was always there on time. The *ezan* in Sarajevo was somehow softer and more beautiful than anywhere else. As I lay in bed in my little *mahala* flat and slept, sometimes fitfully, the sound of *ezan* that came from the little mosque beside my house woke me up like a gentle rain you don't mind getting wet from. I always drifted back into a much sweeter sleep after *sabah,* the dawn prayer. My apartment had a terrace that looked out onto the neighbourhood and made me feel like

I was part of the busy life around me, even if I was just sitting alone. I had French doors that opened on to the terrace and, as I sat, looked out onto the street where I could see the Pržionica, where they roasted coffee in the mornings, its rich smell wafting out, and over the minarets and the rooftops of the houses below mine.

My bathroom had a little window that opened inwards from the bottom and was exactly at street level. It was in the wall above the tub and in the summer, when I took showers, I left the window open so I could look outside. I liked the feeling that I was able to see outside while nobody could detect me through the tiny, secret window at their feet. One day while I was taking a shower a couple walked by my open window. I heard their voices deep in conversation. It had rained and as they walked by my window drops of water dripped off their shoes. I heard the sound of their footsteps fade and began to squeeze some shower gel onto my sponge. I was washing myself with one of those soft sponges that look like a flower and come in all different colours. As I ran my hand down my body I felt something in my left breast.

A very large, hard something.

I wasn't looking for it. I never gave myself breast exams: the UN doctors gave us yearly physicals, which included a breast exam. Breast cancer was not high on my list of worries. High on my list were worries that were much more probable. Like whether I could find a job now that my UN contract had run out. Like how I was going to get my relationship back on track with my boyfriend of four years, not that it had ever been on track. Like, most of all, how I was going to manage to stay in Sarajevo at any cost. And really, why should I have worried about breast cancer? I had no family history and didn't smoke or drink.

As I felt the mass, my mind went back to a day when, as an undergraduate at the University of Toronto, I'd attended a women's health bazaar in the lobby at the Sigmund Samuel Student Centre. I remembered a table that was dedicated to breast cancer. There was a plastic breast in which there were several masses. The woman behind the table had us feel the breast and then made us stop at a tiny, hard, rock-like lump.

"Do you feel that?" she'd asked. "That is malignant. That is cancer."

At that moment, I'd directed myself to store that feeling in my memory for future use. I remembered exactly how it had felt and, in my mind, I now immediately made the comparison. Nope, mine didn't feel the same. It was huge to start with and it wasn't hard like a rock. It moved around and, I thought to myself, if this was cancer, I'd be dead. I dropped my arm, washed out my fluffy sponge, and finished my shower.

I all but forgot about the mass except that it was so big that I couldn't ignore it when I put on my bra or when I instinctively touched my left breast so much more often now that I knew it was there. It wasn't something that had been smaller and had grown. One day it was just there. And it was big. Very big. It took up about half the size of my breast.

I thought: it's nothing. It can't be cancer. But while I didn't admit anything to myself, behind the scenes of my everyday life and relationships a chronic, grey screen of anxiety began to slowly descend. Every time I thought of the mass, my throat and stomach tightened. I kept coming up with all the reasons why breast cancer was impossible. I had no family history, I wasn't a smoker, I had never been seriously sick. I comforted myself with these thoughts, yet I had the nagging feeling that something was wrong.

One day when my friend Maja was staying with me, I asked her to touch my breast. She had been a medical student for five years and I thought that she might say, "It's nothing". When Maja felt my breast I could tell she was horrified, however much she tried to hide it. She asked me, more like begged me, to see a doctor. I finally caved and went to see a gynaecologist. I prayed to God that this was not a sign, an omen that meant I'd have to return to Canada.

A return that I tried more and more desperately to evade the closer it loomed.

I worked at UNHCR in making returns easier; mostly the return of people displaced from their homes during the war. As part of my job, I visited hundreds of families in Bosnia and Herzegovina's villages, where I learned the unavoidable truth that, sooner or later, everybody returns.

One family had returned to the home they'd fled as their village became engulfed in flames. Many of the men had been murdered, tied together with barbed wire, shot and thrown into the river below to drown. Hamza, his wife, and five children had ended up in a refugee camp and, with the help of UNHCR, been resettled in suburban Michigan. Ten days before becoming eligible to apply for green cards, Hamza had packed up his family and returned to live on the charred patch of land that used to be his house. "I just couldn't wait 10 more days," he said. I couldn't believe it. Ten more days? He couldn't have waited 10 more days? Ten more days would have bought his family green cards and a bright future in America. Ten more days would have bought his children lifetimes of possibilities. It seemed somehow so irresponsible, so devil-may-care. I didn't understand.

Or maybe I did.

It took a year after the first gynaecologist in Sarajevo told me that the mass, in his opinion, was cancer, to call home and tell my family that there was something in my breast. I did, but I didn't have the guts to tell them how long it had been there and that I'd visited doctor upon doctor in Sarajevo, only going back to one. That one wasn't a doctor at all, but a "healer", who told me there was nothing wrong with me and gave me some natural remedies to minimise the "fat deposit".

Back in Toronto, during the entire time I was in treatment, I woke up every day with the same consecutive thoughts that played through my mind. Every morning, when I opened my eyes, I was hit by the reality of my illness. Sleep brought me a sweet escape from that reality but it was like groundhog day every morning when I woke up to remember that calamity had visited me. If I was unsure of its proportions, the bald, hairless, bloated head that stared back at me when I looked in the mirror — which was hardly ever — reminded me of the soul-gripping reality that I had cancer. The dreaded disease, our contemporary equivalent of the bubonic plague, the C-word — I had it. I was afflicted. I had been struck down. This was not happening to anyone else, it wasn't a movie, it wasn't a book, it wasn't on *Oprah* — it was my life. It happened to me. This thought pulled me down into a black hole of desperation. I'd forget to breathe and the shorter my breathing became, the more hopeless I felt.

Then the second thought slowly pulled me up. Slowly, inch by inch, like an antidote to a poison that seeped through my veins and was supposed to bring me back to life as it did, the second, glorious, wonderful, beautiful thought restored my breath: I will get better, I will go back. I will get better, I will go back. I will get better, I will go back. Like a soldier's, my mind began marching to the beat of this mantra automatically whenever I felt crushed under the weight of my present. The survival mechanism kicked in before I sank into total despair. As my mind marched, I vividly imagined the streets I would walk, the cafés I would sit in, the tiny corner shops I would visit in Sarajevo. I imagined the face of every waiter at every café where I was a regular and exactly what I would say to him. I imagined exactly what I would be wearing, how I would look, and what I would order. I imagined the friends I would be so happy to see, and the scenarios in which I would see them. Who would come to get me at the airport? How would I feel to, once again, arrive in Sarajevo, the way I had flown in so many times before, to the airport that had greeted me over and over. The memories that my imagination built upon were suddenly bright and alive as though a parallel reality existed in my mind where I truly lived, and reality as I knew it now was a temporary wrench thrown into the story of my life.

I will go back.

6

PEEING RED

I STARTED CHEMOTHERAPY as a newly-jilted 34 year old with long, thick, auburn hair I usually wore down to my waist, a perky set of 36Bs I considered my best asset, and a slight dissatisfaction with the shape of my nose and the generous size of my backside. Back in my Sarajevo life, I plucked my Iranian eyebrows weekly, carefully shaping them into a chestnut arch and then trimming them to perfect the frame. My eyelashes were curled every day before I applied dark blue mascara to enhance my large, almond shaped green-brown eyes that always betrayed me, displaying my true feelings to any spectator and which, along with my hair, were my most complimented physical attributes. I walked down the street rather confident in the fact that I was pretty, flipping my mane of hair over to one side as I walked and felt the stares that followed as my backside, squeezed into leggings or stretchy jeans, attracted the primal attention of expressive Bosnian males. I peered into shop windows I walked by, not to look at the display as I pretended, but to check my reflection at least several times a day.

I had a special relationship with my hairdresser, Kenan, who ooohed and ahhhed as he blow-dried my hair, curling the glossy strands around a big, round brush as he pulled the curl out and let it fall softly around my shoulders in waves that everyone in the salon turned to admire.

"*Gledaj,*" he would exclaim, "*vidi je kosa.*" Look, just look at her hair. I revelled in all that glossy hair that would fall around me section by section, newly coloured, curled and hot from the heat of the hairdryer. At Kens, my cut, colour and blow-dry would be a whole-day affair starting with coffee with the girls while my hair was being coloured to eating lunch at the salon with Ken and the staff who ordered out for sandwiches, and then another coffee as my hair was lovingly blow-dried by Dženana, Kenan's second-in-command or Kenan himself, a theatrical production in which they lavished on my movie-star locks all their attention and expertise.

Kenan was Olja's hairdresser and like all the other services she introduced me to in Sarajevo, it was she who took me there for the first time. Instantly I was part of the inner circle and became a loyal client, using the salon he'd named after himself as my pick-me-up on days I was feeling low and the fuelling station for my elixir of femininity. Kenan had just begun hairdressing school when war broke out and was often unable to make the long trek to college due to shelling and snipers. His happy, positive personality, though, enabled him to earn his credentials by becoming personal hairdresser to the women in his building, cutting and styling in the corridors, eventually attracting women from the neighbourhood to his war-time salon. Olja had been his first client. After the war he opened a real salon in Sarajevo's centre. Kenan, boyishly handsome and endlessly fun, would cut, style, and colour dressed in tight shirts, jeans, and Pumas, his own blond locks gelled to messy perfection. Always sexy and undeniably straight, he danced and sang to music as he worked, admired by his beautiful clientele. Sometimes I'd sit, my hair in foils, and try to imagine him cutting hair during the war, without water or electricity or food for that matter, except for the humanitarian aid that UN planes dropped from the sky containing cans of Spam that had expired 20 years earlier. Before I could picture the scene, he'd look over at me, flash a charming smile, check my foils, and tell one of the girls to wash my hair.

"*Hajmo danas šiške da te skratimo, za malo promijenu.*" How about some bangs this time? Just for a change, Dženana would say, and would use another set of scissors that she dragged across my forehead in a downward pointed straight line, after which I felt edgy and sexy as I shook out my head to reveal a fringe of hair that seductively covered some of my left eyebrow and made my eyes pop. It was a hairstyle that made me instinctively tilt my head coquettishly down while talking or brush the bangs to one side, gently clasped between two fingers. My fringe attracted fingers of appreciation from others, too. Male co-workers, flirts, friends of Man-Boy who secretly harboured a crush, womanisers, opportunists, and other admirers who, during conversations, dared to reach out and brush my fringe aside tenderly, a gesture that always resulted in me blushing and looking down as inside me a glint of happiness shone that I had the power to invoke such moments with a mere shake of my head.

Whenever I left Kens, I always sashayed down Ferhadija, Sarajevo's catwalk flanked by outside cafés, proudly swaying my hips, head held high, crowned by my newly pampered mane of hair that always turned heads after a Kens day. My little power walk made me feel desired and sensual as I drank in the looks of appreciation in the eyes of the waiters and storeowners who stood in the doorways of their establishments and shamelessly stared as I passed. I never looked at them, but my peripheral vision was all attention, checking whether they looked at me. A feeling of victory ensued when I could confirm they had. Those who didn't look or even glance or were occupied elsewhere triggered a sense of anxiety that perhaps I'd lost my powers. I'd panic slightly as I kept walking, making sure that I'd got the majority of men whose paths I crossed to appreciate my curves, my hair, and my strut. Only then, feeling confident and secure in my charms, would I head home.

For my thirty-third birthday, Kenan stayed open late especially to style my hair for the big birthday party I'd planned at Bazeni, one of Sarajevo's clubs. "Curly, Meri, I'm going to give you curls," and he went on, with his assistant, to curl my head of hair.

I had so much hair it took him longer than he'd anticipated and an hour later spiral curls unleashed from their position bounced around my head. We gushed together as he ran his fingers through my hair and positioned each section around my head with bobby pins. I wore a green wraparound dress; meticulously applied makeup blended shades of green eye shadow that made my eyes sparkle under the lights of the club. I opened my presents, ate, and laughed, seated at the head of a long table around which were all the friends I'd collected during my stay.

"*Živjeli Meri!*" my Bosnian friends toasted me. To your long life, may you live 100 years! Around my neck hung a necklace, gold flower dangling from a black and gold ribbon, a surprise gift from Man-Boy, the evening's host, who happily chatted with the guests and held me close for pictures and I glowed with happiness, feeling like a complete woman: loved, befriended, admired and well on the way to crafting the unique, meaningful life I'd always dreamt would be mine. That night a mass of shiny curls danced at my shoulders and I'd never felt more beautiful as I celebrated the last birthday in my city of dreams.

"It's best to shave your head as soon as your hair starts to fall out," advised Tammy the week before I was scheduled for my first round of chemo at Sunnybrook. "You'll start losing clumps after the second round and we suggest you cut your hair really short beforehand — psychologically it's easier to handle if you lose your hair in stages."

Thankfully, I was still protected by the heavy armour of shock which didn't allow her words to fully penetrate my psyche. I simply nodded in a stunned silence. In the span of one month the life I'd been living had vanished and what was left was a place I couldn't recognise, a terrible world, white and empty like a hospital examination room, where my existence hung in the balance and I prepared to sacrifice my body to save my life.

Two days after the second round of chemo, I was surprised by how well I'd been able to withstand the chemical onslaught on my body. I still had my period, still looked like me, but had the appetite of a baby elephant. My hair had been cut into a very chic, French crop that I actually liked and which I pinned to one side with crystal-studded bobby pins I matched to my clothes. I even got compliments from people who, unaware of the reason for my new style, admired my new cut. "You look so sophisticated," they cooed. Maybe chemo wasn't that bad after all said the voice of denial in my head as I trudged farther into this unpredictable new world. Several days after the second round of chemo I stepped into the shower, turned on the taps to adjust the temperature and stood under the hot stream of water for several minutes before reaching for the shampoo. I poured a small amount from the bottle into the palm of my hand, put the bottle down on the bathtub ledge, and began to work my newly cut hair into a foamy lather. I felt a clump of hair come out in my hand.

I froze just long enough for the realisation to dawn on me that chemo was going to be exactly as Tammy had predicted. I was not an exception.

I felt like my heart was going to beat itself right out of my chest. Every single happy scene of the life I'd lived until that moment, as I stood naked and shell-shocked under the shower in my girlhood tub, hit me with the force of a high-speed train. In one second I thought that it wasn't real, couldn't be real, and opened my hand to look down at the thick, healthy, auburn clump I was clutching. As the stream of water hit my head and ran down my body, along with it came more thick, healthy patches of my beautiful hair that until moments ago had been attached to my head, had been part of me, part of who I was, a person I liked, a person I'd worked so hard to be. In that moment, I felt I was losing myself. Gone forever was that happy-go-lucky girl who'd bounced down the street so sure of herself, so sure of the path her life would take, bubbly, warm and trusting, expecting that life would always turn out for the best and that she would always live a charmed existence with only minor bumps and bruises; and as I stood there, motionless, feeling the strands of my hair run down my body, felt all the hair on my groin loosen with the shower's water pressure, sticking to my legs before being washed down my body, I realised that I was becoming someone else. Someone I didn't know and didn't choose; someone whose metamorphosis was beginning with a makeover of chilling proportions. I crouched in my shower and watched my hair disappear down the drain.

Since being diagnosed with cancer I'd shut down any communication with God. As far as I was concerned, I wasn't happy with His recent decisions. Most of my prayers for the last five years had centred on Man-Boy. "Please God, make this work out, let my parents accept him, let him find a steady job, make it so that we can live happily ever after. Please God, please. I love him so much." I could understand how five years of this would have become rather boring to any listener, but the recent turn of events was not exactly how I expected the Creator to answer my prayers – even if the answer was no.

I believed in God. Not only had I been raised learning prayers by heart, I believed in an omnipotent Creator who had always somehow shown me proofs of existence: signs, dreams, a feeling, an omen, when I asked. God was everywhere in Bosnia. One day I went down the street to buy tomatoes and started a conversation with the shop girl, a pretty brunette in her early twenties. She told me she worked six days a week to help support her family and that her father had been killed in the war. "I thank God I have this job. I don't hate anybody; I just want to stay in Sarajevo where my father's bones are buried." Meeting Bosnians who'd survived so much humbled me. It was their belief in God that confirmed mine, a belief that transcended their physical circumstances, that was unconditional. The daily sight of mosques, churches, synagogues, and the sound of the call to prayer made me feel permanently connected to the metaphysical, as if Sarajevo by some divine decree was a window to that world. So I surprised even myself when I froze God out as soon as my life hit a major snag. I didn't pray to get better, didn't ask God to heal me and didn't seek comfort beyond the television screen. I knew that my mother and the rest of my family had kicked into high gear as far as praying for me was concerned. In fact, my mother had enlisted our Jewish relatives in Israel, who sent me a special prayer written for me by their rabbi in the shape of a tiny scroll that I was to pin to myself when I slept. Muslim friends in Iran had buried the bones of a sacrificed lamb, a traditional Shiite invocation to God, asking for my recovery. My Serbian friend across the street had visited Ostrog, a famous Orthodox monastery in Serbia from where she brought me a prayer bracelet and an icon of Saint Vassily, the patron saint of health. My mother asked Baha'i friends travelling to the Baha'i holy places in Israel to remember me in their prayers at the shrines. She herself stayed up half the night chanting prayers I could hear from my bedroom between fits of sobbing that overtook her.

"The chemo is cumulative," said Tammy, meaning that the more I got, the worse it would get. I was scheduled for eight rounds in a four-month period from June to September. Every two weeks I would receive one round of a crimson chemo cocktail that was part of a clinical trial suggested by Dr. Verma and approved by my cousin, Dr. Massoud, a renowned Florida pathologist specialising in breast cancer treatment. Chemo made me pee red and love lamb, a life form whose consumption I'd avoided since birth. The smell of the lamb my grandmother used to cook in our house would wake me from the deepest slumber, mimicking morning sickness, and drive me into the streets until my mother would confirm that all the windows had been opened and my grandmother promised never to cook lamb again when I was home. Surprisingly enough, I even managed to avoid eating lamb during the six years I lived in a Balkan country where lamb on a spit is a delicacy served at weddings, parties and religious holidays. The sight of a skinned lamb roasting over a fire impaled on a metal rod curbed my appetite for 24 hours and I stuck to bread and cabbage salad at any event where lamb was the main course, making sure to sit between two smokers so I could inhale the comforting smell of Marlboro Lights over the smell of lamb that turned my stomach. After my first round of chemo, we drove home and my father parked the car in the driveway where my Serbian neighbour Djurdja was waiting with a pot in her hand.

"Hoćeš li juhu od jagnje Meri?" Do you want lamb broth Meri? she asked me hesitantly, walking up as I slowly made my way out of the car.

I smelled that familiar smell and my brain waited for the stomach lurch. But suddenly my body wanted that lamb broth more than anything. In fact, I would have drunk it out of the pot had I not been doubled over in a chemo-induced stupor. My father took the pot from her and I inhaled the lamb soup at home under the incredulous stares of my parents. My mother called Djurdja and asked her to make more. Thus began my lamb-broth marathon that only ended after my third chemo, the lowest point in my 34-year existence.

One night in July, I woke up hungry and finished the remnants of lamb broth my mother had left beside me. I tried to put the pot back on the nightstand so I could go back to sleep and realised that I didn't have the strength to lift it. I tried again with no success. It was then that I lay back on the bed, and let myself feel just how bad this all was. And for the first time since my diagnosis I broke down and called on God. "If it's going to be like this," I informed the ceiling, "I can't do it anymore. I want out. You win. Just make this end."

I confided this event only to Beks. "You have to think of it like your lifesaving serum," she advised.

Beks was my age and we'd both been diagnosed with cancer on the same day. She had lymphoma, cancer of the lymphatic system, and we started chemotherapy at the same time. We were introduced by a friend of my mother's who thought that, having so much in common, we should become friends. Beks was also a Baha'i girl of Iranian origin and a dentist. She'd just emerged from a divorce and we talked on the phone almost every day. When we planned to meet at a Persian restaurant so we could eat as much as possible in one sitting, our appetites having become priority number one, I was shocked when I laid eyes on her. While I was wearing a wig that itched so much in the summer heat I often reached under it and scratched my head, Beks was a total babe. And not just by chemo standards. She wore sexy Guess jeans, and the right kind of facial hair: eyebrows and eyelashes. Chemo had not given her my mustard-tinged complexion. She also had a mane of long, thick, gorgeous hair. I knew it was a wig. She'd told me about this top-of-the line, human hair wig she'd gotten; otherwise, I would never have known. Beks was the hottest chemo patient I'd ever seen. I was so sweaty in the car on my way home that I just pulled off my wig as I was driving and threw it on the passenger seat. As I looked back up, my eye caught the horrified expression of the driver next to me – a white bald male.

When I stopped looking in the mirror, Beks became my reflection. Looking at her made me feel like things were not so bad. If Beks and I had the same disease and she looked like a Guess model, I was going to be OK. It occurred to me that Beks was fighting this, fighting being defined by the disease, keeping up appearances as part of the fight. I admired her, was in awe of her really, because I was in no shape to be normal. After fighting so hard to stay in Bosnia, to keep my life moving forward against the inevitable, I had no fight left in me. Beks fought for both of us. I lived vicariously through her normality. She lived alone, cooked and cleaned for herself and owned a puppy. No one who looked at her could tell she was sick.

Compared to her, I was a broccoli. Decisions were made by my parents and doctors in consultation with Dr. Massoud and I simply watched, the frozen spectator of my own life. The last conscious decision I made was on the day my father shaved what was left of my hair, a procedure for which he'd readied the clippers he kept for his own grooming, and which had sat in their box in our kitchen like a bomb, silently ticking until that dreadful day of detonation. Sitting under the clippers he set at level 1, I consciously disassociated myself from my body, shutting off the connection that had been such a mainstay of my identity. From then on I lived in my own reality. The bigger, better and much more colourful reality fed by denial, nostalgia, the Balkan music videos I watched on the Internet, and my pricey supply of former Yugoslavia's best gossip rags, trashy magazines and monthly beauty bibles that I bought from our local Serbian store, my new mecca, which carried everything from pickled green peppers to Ariel, washing powder used by Bosnian housewives regardless of ethnicity, purchased in Oakville at double the price of Tide to reproduce the scents of home.

"Why don't you go to the Look Good Feel Better seminar?"

"Look Good Feel Better" was the name of a beauty-and-cosmetics seminar geared to female cancer patients who were struggling with degrees of baldness. I mean, seriously, look good? Feel better? Were people blind? I had no eyebrows, no eyelashes, skin tone that could only be described as light mustard and was bloated beyond recognition. Oh yeah, and I was bald. Unless the Western world decided overnight that the standard of ultimate beauty was ET and not Gisele Bündchen, it was pretty clear that I wouldn't be looking good for some time and I certainly wouldn't feel better anytime soon either, especially if it depended on me looking good. Why this wasn't as totally obvious to the rest of the world as it was to me was astounding. "You should go," urged my friend Shabnam. "I heard they give out a whole box of free makeup, and not just the crappy brands, I heard they give you Vichy stuff."

Free makeup would have motivated the old me to do just about anything. I had been a makeup addict and spent the equivalent of what most women spent on shoes on tubes of mascara and anything that sparkled. Now, though, the new me did not even bother trying. When one of my close friends got engaged, I agreed to go to the annual Toronto wedding show with her, strolling through the convention centre along with thousands of other newly engageds sporting long-awaited sparkly rings on their left hands and that look of triumph mixed with relief that not even a presidential win can produce. We stopped at the hair-extension display table and the girls at the booth stopped giggling as they watched two women, one bald and rather yellow, approach their area. The manager of the gigglers, a tiny girl with huge, round breasts attempting to free themselves from the confines of a tight red sweater, lowered her voice and addressed me apologetically. "Uh, you actually need to have hair for these extensions."

"When the Lord closes a door, somewhere He opens a window," Maria chirped in *The Sound of Music*, my mother's favourite movie musical, which we'd watched so often I'd memorised the lines. My window during that summer of 2007 was my nails. For all the destruction chemo left in its wake, the effect of the cocktail, for reasons no medical professional could explain, gave me the strongest, fastest growing nails I'd ever had. Every week I had a manicure to enhance the only female attribute I had left. I went all out. I asked the Vietnamese girl who gently filed my nails to give me all manner of little designs on top of the coat of bold polish: flowers, bees, angels adorned with sparkles which I proudly displayed at my hospital appointments.

"Wow, your nails always look so nice," noticed Tammy. I looked down at them, so perfectly polished and so out of place on me, an alien life form with no other sign of actually ever having been a woman.

I used to be pretty; really, you would have thought I was pretty, a voice inside me cried out whenever I saw Dr. Verma, perfunctorily undressed for him and felt him touch my breasts with an open hand, checking whether the tumour had shrunk after every round of chemo. Dr. Verma was young, I'd say about my age, and had we met under different circumstances, like law school or at a party, we would have been friends. I'm sure he would have appreciated me even more in my pre-cancer state and every time I saw him I wished with all of my being that he could have known me then, in my prime, when I would have flirted with him, danced with him, and never let him fondle my breasts without at least some kind of commitment.

The Street of Good Fortune

I confess that I owe one of my breasts to Father Pucci.

Once I'd decided to restore some form of relationship with God, my friend Lucia, a devout Catholic, invited me to Italian mass. The idea of God being worshipped in Italian amidst a congregation of people I didn't know was somehow comforting. As we entered the church, Lucia told me that she'd informed Father Pucci that I was coming and he wanted to meet me before mass. Father Pucci was in his nineties, had come from Italy as a young priest, and had baptised and first-communioned Lucia. Lucia's sister had developed breast cancer at 31, a year after her wedding, which I'd attended. After chemotherapy and radiation, her doctors had urged her to have her ovaries removed, fearing that her type of cancer would attack there next. She'd refused, harbouring the hope of one day having a child. Two years later, her doctors' worst fears were confirmed when the cancer returned and then spread. Lucia lost her sister while I was in Sarajevo and had sought comfort and strength in her faith and Father Pucci. A tiny man with white hair and a great sense of humour, he greeted me in the church office and told me that after mass he would lead the congregation in a special prayer for me. I tried to fight back tears. We knelt in the church and when Lucia whispered, "He's praying for you," I let go and begged God to let me keep my breast.

"Please God; I know I've been AWOL but please just let me keep my breast. Please."

It was a silent prayer but somehow Father Pucci, the man who'd moved me, also moved the Almighty. After agonising months in which I tried to prepare myself for a mastectomy of my left breast, an event I found so horrible that it made me forget death, Dr. McCready decided I could keep my breast. Frankly, given the havoc it had wreaked in my life, I was surprised how desperately I fought for it. My mastectomy turned into a lumpectomy and when Dr. McCready sat on the bed facing me in the pre-op room to draw with a thick black marker the path his scalpel would take on my breast, my vanity was obvious.

"They tell me you're Michelangelo," I joked weakly.

He smiled wryly. "Well, I wouldn't say that," everything about him assuring me that he would, indeed, live up to the hype.

While I was told that chemo would affect my hormones and therefore my mojo, my intense crush on the super-brainy radiation oncologist of Polish descent proved that my hormones were no shrinking violets. Balkanised by six years of ingesting *kajmak* (clotted cream) and *kiseli kupus* (pickled cabbage), it would take a lot more than chemo to keep them down. Dr. Czarnota was Sunnybrook's genius extraordinaire. With about 12 letters following the MD after his name, and his own lab where he and a team of physicists worked on different ways of improving cancer treatment, I wondered whether he was a direct descendant of Marie Curie. Sunnybrook's blond, blue-eyed superstar was tall, Slavic, and painfully shy. Though he was 39, he spiked his hair with gel and blushed a lot like an awkward schoolboy. For someone with his achievements and talent, he was extremely humble and answered all of my parents' questions with patience, which, believe me, was no small feat. A tall, Polish (almost Bosnian) genius who spent his days finding the cure for cancer: not just any cancer but a cancer that only afflicted women. Hello. I was totally hooked. While most of my friends thought that it was a common patient/healer phenomenon to fall in love with your doctor, had I not been his patient and had Victoria's Secret sold radioactive lingerie, he and I would have walked happily together into the sunset. I knew I was exactly the kind of woman he needed: bubbly and hyper, just the kind of girl to bring him out of his shell. By the time I was seeing Dr. Czarnota on a regular basis, I had about one inch of hair and therefore was, as far as I was concerned, smoking hot. Despite my wardrobe of men's sweats, I wore eyeliner on every visit and was devastated when his resident showed up to check the burns on my breast instead of him. He was there on my very first radiation visit, though and, despite the presence of my parents, when he drew the curtain between them and us to see the results of my breast surgery, I sat up tall on the examination table, happily untied my robe and sucked in my stomach. Despite the fact that I had a four-inch scar across my left breast, I was sure I was his hottest patient. I mean I was probably one of his youngest patients. Even though Dr. McCready's surgery had left my left breast slightly smaller than the right one, it was exactly the same shape, and perkier now. So I untied, let my gown fall away with pride and looked up at him. I expected to catch a glint of appreciation in his eyes or at least some intense blushing but instead he looked horrified.

"You decided against a mastectomy?" he asked with dismay.

"Uh, well, uh, yesss."

I had to breathe out to answer and the extra weight I was carrying around my waist made its appearance. Clearly I wasn't going to get anywhere using my feminine wiles. I was never the kind of girl to throw out my breasts or be overtly sexual in my attempts to attract men but I wasn't opposed to a little décolleté and cleavage was pretty high up in my flirting arsenal. I knew some men were leg men or butt men but I had never been up against a man who wished I had fewer breasts.

It was a challenge I was up to though, because he was just so achingly cute in all his nervous awkwardness. Unfortunately, Dr. Czarnota never did come around. I could only chalk it up to his extreme respect for our doctor/patient relationship and the fact that he thought litigation could cause him to lose his job and professional licence and seriously get in the way of revolutionary medical advances he was working on, costing millions of lives.

It made me dig him even more.

7

NO HOMES AND NO FAMILIES

THE WINTER I was in radiation my friend Beca and her father Mirza visited me. Beca and I had lived in the same graduate students' dorm at university. When I first met her she was watching *Sherlock Holmes*, then my favourite show, on A&E, a channel I was able to watch because I was an only child and therefore the sole commander of the remote control. Beca was also an only child and we watched TV late at night when all the giggling girls had gone to bed and we could indulge our common yen for intelligent television programming. She would smoke Marlboro Lights inside, back in the days when it was legal, and we'd watch through the screen of smoke that she produced as she worked through the half-empty pack of cigarettes she kept on the couch beside her.

Beca was from Sarajevo and she was the first Bosnian I ever met. She was the child of the retired director of a Yugoslav utility company and his wife, a judge, and she was adopted.

When Beca's parents were unable to have a child, her father called upon his brother, the Chief of Staff of Sarajevo's hospital, to help them adopt a baby boy. Beca was the one-year-old, sickly child lying in the crib beside the healthy, newborn baby boy that Mirza's brother had delivered himself. When Beca's mother opened the door to her husband, fully expecting him to be carrying a male heir, handpicked by destiny to carry on their name, she was amazed to come face to face with an almost-toddler of the opposite sex. Legend has it that when Mirza bent over the baby boy's crib, Beca caught his attention. As he turned to look at her, she reached out and clutched the finger of the six-foot-four giant, who at that moment decided that pink and not blue would be the colour of his dynasty.

I loved this story. I used to ask Beca to tell it to me sometimes when we met, like a little child requesting a beloved bedtime story, a request she obliged, always between puffs of Marlboro Lights and gulps of coffee. Often this story would be interrupted by calls from Mirza himself, ensuring that all was well and dispensing advice about whatever activity we were engaged in at the time.

"Eat the squid," he commanded from Canada as Beca and I sat in a restaurant on the Croatian coast, not far from her summer house. "And ask for the curly-haired waiter; tell him you're Mirza's."

"*Dobro Tata, dobro*," she would placate him; OK dad, OK. And we ordered the squid and ogled the curly-haired waiter while our waiter served us cold coffees with a sneer because Beca didn't want to be rude. To me, Mirza was a superman.

He certainly was the biggest man I'd ever seen and the first time I met him, in his Toronto apartment, he made me kiss a bust of Marshal Tito he kept by the door. He lived by the principles that had shaped him and refused to sell out, like so many others of his circle, who changed their political allegiances to suit their bank accounts. I admired this in him but what I admired most was the story that connected him to Beca and inspired me more than ever during the long winter days of radiation. He made me believe that I, too, could have such a story. And I could, but I needed his help. When Mirza and Beca visited me in that cold, bleak January, it was the only thing on my mind. He sat in my kitchen and I, so unwell, made him cold Nescafé, which he sipped politely. Mirza's size was so overwhelming that the look in his eyes when I opened the door and he saw me bald, ashen, and wearing grey, baggy flannel pyjamas, surprised me. A look of shock and then intense pain flashed across his face and took refuge in his eyes, where it remained during the whole visit no matter how much he smiled. His attempt to veil his distress at seeing his daughter's friend hovering dangerously close to death was obvious and, like a true father, he began to normalise the situation by dispensing advice, a monologue I interrupted.

"Mirza, when I get better can you help me get a Bosnian passport?"

Mirza had connections, friends, relatives back in Bosnia who could help me legalise the five years I'd lived in the country into a residency permit that could become citizenship.

"Meri, for what?"

Bosnian citizenship was no coveted prize. He thought it was a nostalgic, sentimental request. I never worried about Bosnian citizenship while I was there because I assumed that once I married Man-Boy I would automatically be eligible. But now I needed connections and a good lawyer to get citizenship. Mirza was my best shot.

"Meri," he told me, "*polako* (all in good time)." He changed the subject and invited me to stay at his summer house on the sea, recovering under the Dalmatian sun. I loved his summer house and the Dalmatian sun, but my goal that day was something else. I told him my reason.

"Mirza, only Bosnian citizens can adopt Bosnian children and so I need a passport."

I was shocked when he began to cry.

"Meri, *sine*, think of your health, just think of your health."

And he slowly wiped his face with an open palm, starting at his forehead and covering his eyes for many moments before moving his hand down to his chin and back to his lap.

Bosnia's orphans were subject to quite a deliberate class system. High-class were the orphans lucky enough to live at the swish Swiss outfit, SOS Kinderdorf, restricted to children who had lost their parents in the war. These kids lived in clean, newly-built "children's villages" with playgrounds and houses that included a "mother" and an "aunt", women who had no children of their own and were thus in a position to devote all their love and attention to the four children placed under their care in each house. Middle-class were the children living in orphanages supported by the church. One of my flats in Sarajevo overlooked the Ljubica Ivezić orphanage, made famous in the movie *Welcome to Sarajevo* and thereafter supported by a Montreal diocese of the Catholic Church. I could hear the children in their gymnasium on Sunday mornings, singing hymns during mass. The bottom-rung, most populous class of orphans was housed in the now dilapidated state-run institutions that for years had been home to forgotten children. Children from unfortunate backgrounds with even more unfortunate parents, many of whom had themselves been raised in institutions: children who actually got more food and better clothes when war broke out and they suddenly became visible to foreign donors, confirming the fact that orphans in war fare better than orphans in peace. In Bosnia, anyway.

My first love, my biggest passion, and the only meaningful work endeavour in my Being Christiane Amanpour life was not a glam UN post but a make-work project of my own invention at the Home and Families in Zenica, central Bosnia's industrial armpit. Despite that fact, I held a deep affection for Bosnia's pre-war, now depressed centre of steel production. Aesthetics aside, the true beauty of Bosnia is that every city has a soul and Zenica is no different. This sad-looking grey city built on a beautiful, green patch of the country was my backdrop for irretrievable moments of bitter-sweetness and people who will never return to me. My memories existed in a sepia-coloured mist that surrounded them like tissue paper wrapped around fragile, precious objects gingerly placed in gift boxes. Memories the colour of longing; the colour of negatives from my interrupted childhood in a foreign land, captured in tiny plastic slides I would look through as a child trying to remember the feelings frozen in the film.

Every Saturday I would pack up the small red stick-shift Volkswagen hatchback I learned how to drive in Sarajevo, pick up my friend Alma, and make the 70-km trek to the orphanage, *Dom i Porodica*, the Home and Families, to teach the kids English, take them to parks, and attempt to make their lives brighter, if only for a nanosecond. Truth be told, I was much more ambitious, thinking that Alma and I could suddenly transform these small inhabitants of life's darkest, dirtiest places into MENSA candidates. Alma, more realistic and also fluent in the language, had her doubts.

"Meri, they think we're spies," she whispered as the "pedagogue" walked by, all stiff hairspray and purple lips, dressed with impeccable care in what looked like a Cruella de Ville costume.

The pedagogue was something like a staff counsellor, a title left over from socialist times, which meant little other than that such a staff member must be employed according to the state's human resources formula for orphanages. The staff at the Home and Families was not welcoming. I was oblivious, mostly because at that time my Bosnian was still rudimentary.

"Meri, they think you are a spy and I am your interpreter. They think that you are here from OHR to spy on what they are doing."

The Street of Good Fortune

This was hilarious to me for several reasons. The OHR or Office of the High Representative was the postwar UN-established body that oversaw Bosnia and Herzegovina's political structure, headed at the time by a one-time German diplomat presiding over an outrageously overpaid international staff.

Not that any of that really mattered though because, unfortunately for the kids at Home and Families, they did not come within a 100-km radius of OHR's "mandate" and, even more unfortunately for me, I was not collecting a six-figure euro, tax-free OHR salary. My treks to Zenica with crayons, paper, balloons and snacks were funded by my Visa Gold card that I had proudly accepted upon law-school graduation, and now made me feel like I could actually afford the expenses I was racking up. The paranoid suspicion of the H and F staff only went to show how precious little the Bosnian rank and file actually knew about the confusing map of international organisations that had arrived in their country to save them from themselves. Alma and I persisted at the orphanage despite the suspicion that shadowed us.

Home and Families, a misnomer of colossal proportions, was an old, low-rise, Soviet-style block structure made up of five floors, each with a series of large apartments. Each apartment included a lounge area, kitchen and bathroom as well as four bedrooms where the children slept, up to four to a room. Apartments called "families" were home to about 12 children according to inexplicable criteria. It wasn't based on family relationships, though, because, strangely enough, siblings were never placed together in one "family".

Each family had a "*vaspitač*", an "educator", a term that encompassed a spectrum of individuals from the mentally ill to the quasi-criminal. This was mostly because all manner of people stomped over each other to get jobs as educators since, on top of the salary and health insurance the job secured, it also came with a one- or two- bedroom apartment, utilities included, in the Home and Families building. Unlike the apartments where the children were housed, these were reserved for the educators and their own biological families based on generally accepted bonds of kinship. At 18, children were kicked out of the Home and Families while the children of the educators were allowed to stay as long as their parents had the job. This was, incidentally, and maybe not so incidentally, the same institution where my Man-Boy and his siblings grew up.

Separated in different families.

Naturally.

"Grew up", of course, is a relative term. My Man-Boy's sister, Seka, was kicked out of Home and Families before the war for being "troubled". At 15, she was transferred to an institution for "troubled" girls four hours away from her brothers. Man-Boy told me that he refused to let anyone else bathe him for weeks since, on top of being troublesome, Seka managed to ensure that her younger brothers were bathed, fed, and defended from the institution's bullies, who feared her wrath. Several years later, in the middle of the war, my then 14-year-old Man-Boy was ejected from Home and Families by Aida, the institution's director, because he'd had the audacity, in a moment of patriotic fervour, to run away to join his brother, a conscript in the wartime Bosnian army. Upon his repentant return, the director told him that she didn't believe he could re-adjust to life in the orphanage after having been gone for such a long period — two whole weeks. Man-Boy told me stories of the educators' pasts that made my blood boil. I set out upon a quest to expose these transgressions, as though it would make a difference. I made phone call upon phone call to UNICEF and all the NGOs that had a children's programme mandate. One well-known NGO I called to report that the computers they'd donated to the orphanage were only being used by the educators and their families and then locked up so the children wouldn't have access to them actually reported my phone call to the H and F director, who banned me from seeing the children for several weeks. Things improved when I started appearing with Man-Boy, who vouched for me and assured them that, as an Iranian and his new love interest, I couldn't possibly be a spy for OHR's Western powers.

Before I ever met Man-Boy my bond with Home and Families was cemented through Irfan. I first saw Irfan in the orphanage playground the summer before I actually moved to Bosnia, when I travelled through the country with an international dance troupe that happened to perform at the Home and Families. The kids sat behind the building in the playground, a sea of children of all different sizes and ages fidgeting excitedly in the summer heat. They wore colourful, ill-fitting clothes, obviously donations; the best of which I later found out were reserved for the educators' own children. He wore a red t-shirt and green cargo pants that were rolled up several rolls too many.

I noticed his eyes before anything else. They were large and a particular shade of blue. A striking, aquamarine shade I'd only ever seen in the Balkans. They were the same shade of blue I remembered staring at me from the wartime footage of Srebrenica, the last of Bosnia's wartime safe havens, whose fall took with it thousands of boys and men lined up in front of the buses that were taking them to be slaughtered. I remembered being struck by the colour of their eyes as they stood there wondering where those buses would take them. I saw those eyes at Home and Families, eyes that told stories, eyes haunted by history and deep like the colour of the Bosnian sky in summer when you gazed at a horizon that engulfed you in a palpable majestic glow. I claimed Irfan the moment I saw him because he looked up at me with those eyes, half 11-year-old rebel, half vulnerable child.

Irfan was from Velika Kladuša, a town in Northern Bosnia known mostly for an unsuccessful attempt in the war to separate from the central command in Sarajevo and become a territory run by Fikret Abdić, the owner of AgroKomerc, an agricultural company in which most of Velika Kladuša's inhabitants worked. Having established a prosperous business empire in a socialist country, one that supported hundreds of families and relied on friendly relations between Bosnia and neighbouring Croatia, Abdić had tried to maintain those relations with the Croatian government while the two countries were at war — high treason to Sarajevo's central command. Velika Kladuša soon started to war against central command as well as Croatia. Abdić was captured as a war criminal and AgroKomerc became a fond memory for a region that became mired in conflict and poverty. Rumour had it that, after the war, Irfan's father, mother, uncle and aunt killed a gypsy woman for 100 KM, Konvertibilni Marks, the equivalent of about $70. The whole family was arrested and incarcerated, the men in Zenica's KP Dom, the maximum security prison, and the women in Tuzla's women's prison three hours away from Zenica. The seven children went to Home and Families.

I sat beside him, talking in a mixture of English and my nascent Bosnian mostly extracted from a tiny yellow pocket dictionary. Before I left the orphanage to continue with our tour of his country, Irfan gave me a small pink stuffed bear, one of his few possessions. "To remember me by," he explained when I protested. Back in Canada after my trip, I kept in touch with him through letters I exchanged with many of the Home's children. But when I returned months later it was Irfan who I was most eager to see. Irfan was H and F's resident bad-boy, misunderstood, often aggressive, and with scant respect for authority. The staff had given up on him and established a policy of containment, spiced, depending on the day and the educator, by cruel comments and humiliation.

A policy completely disrupted by my arrival.

I indulged him. I bought him fake Nikes that looked almost real from Zenica's open market and took him out to eat at fast-food restaurants. I gave him five marks whenever I saw him and made him swear to me he wouldn't buy cigarettes.

"Buy something nice for Zlata."

Zlata was the eldest of Irfan's three younger sisters and they often fought.

"She's your sister," I would always say, trying to cultivate whatever bond was left between them, "it's your job to take care of your sisters. You're the oldest."

He looked at me with those eyes and they told me that he would, if he only knew what to do, if he could only get a break, prove himself outside the military regimen that reigned at the orphanage, where no one was ever given the benefit of the doubt, where every act was questioned, and encouragement was reserved for days when American evangelists visited to distribute Bibles to the children and cash to the staff.

I understood.

I saw bits of myself in him. He was wild and transparent, emotional and uncalculating and raw.

Unusual in someone who'd grown up in his circumstances, Irfan had virtually none of the invisible protective layer that often resulted from a fleeting childhood. When many of the other children tuned out the hurtful words directed at them by the staff, Irfan would be physically affected.

"You're going to end up just like your father," one of the educators predictably told him.

He reeled as though he'd been struck. I felt the sting in his eyes. Mine, too, went shiny and burned.

"Don't listen to them," I told him. "They are evil."

"So is my father," he would retort.

This vulnerability in him scared me. It scared me that he would continue in a life that would only become harder without a thick skin necessary to survive it. He would sit obediently beside me as I chastised him quietly for his most recent transgression.

"Meri, I can't help it," he once told me. "It's like I just see black and I can't control myself."

I couldn't help but think that, in different circumstances, he would have thrived. I blamed myself for not being able to be a true mother to him, for not making an *Oprah* show-worthy success story out of the relationship I'd forged with him. Like him, I would have if I'd only known what to do, if I could have been less emotional, more reasonable; if I'd planned a different life, a life with a plan, a plan that included a long-term solution for Irfan, for his sisters, for all of them, for myself. But, as it was, I lived day to day like a guilty single parent overcompensating for my lack of planning with trips to hamburger joints and the cafés that served his favourite pastries.

When Irfan turned 15, the orphanage hatched a plan to get rid of him, as they did with many children they simply couldn't be bothered to deal with anymore. The same plan that sent my Seka to the school for "troubled" girls saw Irfan transferred to a similar home for delinquents in Sarajevo. On one hand he was happy; the move brought him closer to me. I got a call from the pedagogue one summer day in my flat with high ceilings on Čekaluša Čikma in Sarajevo's peaceful Mejtaš district.

"Irfan will be moving to Sarajevo to a new home."

I knew all about this plan. Man-Boy had already explained it to me. Man-Boy was jealous of the attention I lavished on Irfan and Irfan warned me incessantly about Man-Boy.

"Meri, why him? Of all the guys why him?"

I thought it was just adolescent jealousy but later wondered if Irfan had seen something I didn't with those eyes that had seen far too much.

I called him *sine,* son, a term of endearment reserved for your own child or any child you felt was your own.

"*Sine,*" I would ask, "*jesi li gladan?*" Are you hungry?

He was always hungry, a growing Balkan boy, and we ate together at the pizza place across from the National Theatre and VF Komerc, a supermarket with a buffet. Then we would walk through the supermarket and I'd buy him soap and shampoo and Axe aftershave spray since he was now trying to impress a girl at his new school.

"What's her name?" I asked him.

The Street of Good Fortune

"Selma," he blushed, looking down with a mixture of pleasure and embarrassment.

Her name was Selma, the same as one of his sisters. I often thought of bringing Irfan and his sisters to live with me. That way they would be together and we could be a family. But my contracts were all for six months or less and I had no house. I did daydream of a time when I would save money, get a house, and maybe start my own orphanage where I would move all the kids from Home and Families. A dream with a very small window of opportunity, something I wished I had known back then. I would often give him money for a taxi if we'd been together in town but he always just kept the five or 10 KM bill in his pocket and hung off the back of a tram as it made its way to his new neighbourhood behind the bus station.

One particular night, an ordinary night in a place where everything was extraordinary, I had to cut our outing short. I forget why. We parted as we had so many times before and I saw him walk away in the mist that often infused Sarajevo at night and blurred the line between real and imaginary. We left Café Ramiz after an evening snack of pastry and lemonade for him and cappuccino for me. I rarely went to Café Ramiz, where I found the coffee too bitter and the pastries too sweet, but Irfan liked it. I gave him five marks as we parted and he walked away from me into the mist. At one exact moment he turned around and faded into the night, my Irfan with the big, piercing blue eyes, war eyes, already 15, taller than the child I'd first met, but still prone to tears when talking about his father or being reprimanded by me, left to catch a tram, hanging off the back.

It was the last time I saw him.

The next day I received a phone call from his new *vaspitać*, Hadžo, a kind, gentle man who, weeping, told me that Irfan was dead. Killed by a butterknife through the heart at the hands of another inmate, a disturbed, severely abused child who'd asked Irfan for a cigarette and, when refused, stabbed my boy in the chest, a random, thoughtless movement that could have resulted in a mere flesh wound but had sliced so exactly into the centre of Irfan's heart that even the autopsy doctors were surprised by its precision.

Did I love him like my own?

I never met the woman who did. I wasn't the one who felt him inside me before he was born, kicking and wriggling to get out. He was headstrong and impulsive so I'm sure he was the kind of baby who moved a lot, impatient to see the world. I wasn't the one to give birth to him, naturally since epidurals are only a fantasy in Bosnian hospitals. I didn't hold him to my breast during nightly feedings, groggy and exhausted from the sleeplessness, or help him take his first steps or feed him baby food I'd blended from mashed peas and carrots. I wasn't there when he teethed or when he got a fever to soothe him back to sleep, or hold his hand and take baby steps with him down the street on our way to buy fruits and vegetables at the outdoor market.

The Street of Good Fortune

Irfan never talked about his mother. Irfan's younger sister, Zlata, his only sibling allowed to attend the funeral, sighted her in a police car close to the cemetery. No one could confirm this and, anyway, according to Islamic tradition, women did not attend burials, staying back at the house to pray in the *tevhid* ceremony. At his burial I walked behind his father, who was handcuffed and held up on either side by police guards. The guards whispered consoling sounds to him as they looked down and held their hats in their free hands out of respect for the dead.

In my mind, I already hated Irfan's father. Irfan told me once about how, when he was very small, his father had often beat him, which later required the orphanage doctor to regularly inject him with cortisone to ease the pain in his back. This was why he used to stand always with one hand on his hip, wordlessly shifting his weight back and forth from one leg to another. But when I saw his father for the first time, he looked so much like Irfan, the same huge, Balkan-blue eyes, that the hate which had begun in my head couldn't work its way down to nest in my heart, no matter how hard I tried. Instead, as we slowly walked to the plot of land that had already been prepared for Irfan's body, wrapped in a white shroud as dictated by Islamic burial rites, on a wet, foggy, overcast day, I looked at one of the guards and repeated "*molim* (please)," until he heard me and turned around. I offered the guard the picture of Irfan I held in my hands. It was the last picture taken of him, leaning on the sofa in his Home and Families living room with a smile on his face and those eyes looking across at someone or something. The smile on his lips was overshadowed by the look in his eyes, somewhere between haunting and tragic; but not sad. It was an expression I would see again, in another life, and wonder where I remembered it from. It was a picture of a boy on the cusp of manhood, all adolescent muscles and gangly arms with hands that were older than his face and emanating the scent of youth, a scent of aftershave and anticipation.

A picture of someone who couldn't possibly be dead.

The police guard looked at me and then down at the picture and uttered the inmate's name, motioning me with his head. Irfan's father, who was staring aimlessly down at the ground with a grimace of pain frozen on his face, looked back at me in a daze of grief. I understood that the guard wanted him to take his son's picture from me with his own hands and slowed down so that Irfan's father could turn around and, working around the handcuffs, grasp the picture between the thumbs and first fingers of both hands. The guard looked at me, a silent thank you in his eyes, and we kept slowly trudging in the rain in a line of mourners who were by now used to this far too common ritual as if delivering their young to the gods they'd unknowingly invoked.

I never wept for Irfan. On autopilot, I carefully folded my memories of him and put them away somewhere I knew they'd remain untouched and from where they wouldn't touch me.

After Irfan's death my trips to the orphanage became less and less frequent. When I did go it was more out of a sense of duty to his little sisters than anything else. They all had their brother's eyes and when I saw those eyes gazing at me from a face that wasn't Irfan's, the feeling it gave me had to be immediately diverted to the dark cellar of my psyche as it passed from my eyes to my brain for fear of what it would do to me if left alone to travel to its true destination. Zlata, nearing adolescence, began running away from the Home and Families. Our trips to Zenica turned into search parties where, acting on information from friends and neighbours, we hunted her down under bridges and in gypsy districts.

"Give me 24 hours and I can find anyone in Zenica," boasted my Man-Boy and I believed him until one Sunday night when she was nowhere to be found. After searching every place we'd ever found her in the past, we returned to Sarajevo. For months afterwards I asked the educators if she'd returned or if they were searching for her, a 13-year-old girl alone in the world. Nobody had seen her and nobody cared.

"They didn't even report her missing to the police!" I wailed, to which Man-Boy replied, "Meri, she's not the first and she won't be the last".

I couldn't help thinking that things would have been different had I never arrived. The road to hell apparently travels through Zenica.

Was it then that I stopped thinking of being a mother? Every now and then, on the rare occasions I accompanied Man-Boy back to his home town, I would see the children in the street or outside a store, the same children I'd hugged and kissed back in those months before the funeral. It wasn't the same. I greeted them mechanically, full of the contrived emotion they detected. I felt nothing. No more intense desire to put things right. No more sense of mission to make a difference. Often I felt annoyed that they were there, in front of me, forcing me to act, forcing me to remember them.

I remembered them many, many months later in a white examination room that would have been infinitely more disturbing without the presence of the brown-skinned Dr. Verma, whose head and hands, the only parts of him not covered by a white coat, comforted me in the small, unfamiliar room in which my memories, the horrible, hidden memories I'd worked so hard to erase, came flooding out, fully exposed in the harsh artificial light.

"You may not be able to have children after the chemo, Maryam," said Dr. Verma's steady, gentle voice and all of me broke into a million tiny shards of sadness held together for so long by the unreliable glue of denial that still sometimes cut me in deep places I couldn't otherwise reach.

8

I Have A Scar, A Big Scar Across My Left Breast

On the day of my last appointment with my surgeon Dr. McCready, when, after months of treatment, he told me with what I could swear was a tear in his eye that my tests showed a "phenomenal" result, that I was completely cancer-free, the new me was completely terrified. She had no idea what to do with herself.

"You need a man," stated my friend Holly one day on the phone.

"A what?" I asked.

"A man."

Ah yes, surviving cancer meant that once again I was followed by the ever-present spectre of the place in a woman's life that must, by some cruel law of the universe, be filled by a man. The man question had been in suspended reality since the night before my first round of chemotherapy when Man-Boy had dumped me over the phone. The over-the-phone part I couldn't really hold against him. It was not as if he could very well have flown over so he could dump me face to face. But what shocked me was just how little he'd prepared for the goodbye speech that ended our relationship. It was, by any culture's standards, extremely lame. So lame in fact that I was embarrassed to repeat it to friends when they inevitably asked me when he would be arriving to hold my hand through the next months of what they viewed as the worst part of my life and, obviously, the time when I needed him most.

"Ah, we're not together anymore," I would answer and then slowly proceed to explain the mortifying details to their stunned faces. Man-Boy had begun the dumping with "It's not another girl…" and ended it with "I'm getting on the bus now".

This was the last I heard from the boyfriend with whom I'd spent five years sharing ups and downs.

Mostly my ups and his downs.

I am a fixer, saver girlfriend. I will only be with you if I believe that you are somehow broken and I can reap the rewards of having put you back together again. My insight to you if you recognise yourself in this sentence is that you are projecting. Projecting your own brokenness onto someone else so that you can fix what is outside of you instead of fixing what ails you. It's always infinitely easier to fix someone else and generally speaking there is always a reward, short-lived as it may be. The fixer boyfriend will reward you with gratitude for some time but this relationship will always end in him resenting you for having fixed him, if you succeed, and then a recession back to brokenness as a rebellion against the control you have over his life for having fixed it. It's a lose-lose relationship pattern because you end up drained and maybe with breast cancer and he ends up back where he was when you decided to fix him.

Usually nowhere.

A big waste of time is had by all but at least you look like a great hero that saved an ungrateful "*čisti luzer*", total loser, and many coffees will be drunk by friends and acquaintances attesting to all of the selfless efforts you made to make the *čisti luzer* a man, only to be rewarded by _____ (insert some calamitous event) during which he turns his back on you. It's textbook and yet, for me, always magnetic. It's like somewhere in my subconscious my dream-man list says 1) broken 2) somehow sad and charismatic 3) broke.

No matter how *čisti* a *luzer* my Man-Boy was, I was in love and when I was in love I immediately painted pictures in my mind. Like a pig wallowing in the mud of denial I dreamt up all kinds of happy scenes of a life with him where I wrote, directed and co-starred in an impossible screenplay that could, for a million and one reasons, never happen. Scenes of all kinds of happy moments with him in the male lead repeating all the lines I'd written with the scenery I'd chosen in the exact sequence that I envisioned.

Scenes of eating dinner together in a warm little kitchen with a window overlooking Sarajevo's old town. Scenes of walking down Ferhadija, the main pedestrian thoroughfare, hand in hand, while he pushed the stroller in which our little mixed-marriage baby slept as we said hello to other couples and sat to drink coffee and eat baklava at one of Sarajevo's sweet corner cafés. Scenes of how happy we would be, where he would become exactly the kind of man for whom I'd written this play.

"You need a man to get your hormonal juices flowing again."

A man.

The image that popped into my head when she said it was of a doctor. I couldn't help it. For the last 18 months the only eligible men with whom I'd had relationships wore white coats and spent their time with me fondling my breasts. Because I am Iranian and because we, as a people, are talented in drawing high drama into the most unlikely situations, as fate would have it my line-up of doctors during cancer treatment turned out to be a parade of attractive men under 40. When, after my last round of chemo, I contracted a red-herring, viral strain of pneumonia and had to be hospitalised, a seemingly endless stream of male attending physicians from all backgrounds and cultures, one more eligible and attractive than the last, spent their time at my bedside. My mother, also at my bedside, was beside herself.

"Finally, some decent men, and look where we are!" *EEN HAM SHANSE SIAHE MAN!*

In Farsi this means "My rotten luck!" I thought this was more MY rotten luck than hers, but being the only child and a girl, I was used to sharing luck with my mother. I myself had, as they say in Bosnia, *digla ruke,* given up. I had long ago stopped looking in the mirror and knew that I looked like a very bad version of Sigourney Weaver in the *Alien* movies. In one word: frightening. I kept no pictures of this state. With the advent of Facebook, the lawyer in me decided that such evidence should not be floating around to remind me or anyone else of how I looked during those months. It was something I never wanted to remember. I used to feel sorry for my family and friends who came to visit and the way they hid the shock of seeing me for the first time as a cancer patient. As difficult as it was for me, I couldn't imagine how it felt for the people who loved me.

Of course I daydreamed about meeting a man who would see the true essence of who I was and fall in love with me despite my striking resemblance to ET. Friends of my mother recounted to me the urban legends about how their hairdresser's sister had breast cancer and her boyfriend proposed to her during chemotherapy with a three- carat Tiffany diamond, or about the doctor in LA who fell in love with his chemo patient and married her in Hawaii. But I could still only identify with Kylie Minogue, who beat breast cancer and then had no one to fertilise her frozen eggs. I realised that this was probably not the point in my life where I was going to make any kind of dent in the dating scene so I had already let go of my physical identity and simply decided to be patient and wait for better times in the man sweepstakes. *Biće bolje* they say in Bosnia, it will be better. So simple and yet full of depth and wisdom. Bosnians use this expression when things are especially bad and there doesn't seem to be a way out.

I could imagine people sitting in their flats or houses or in the trenches, with grenades exploding around them and the sound of gunfire incessantly ripping through the air. I could imagine mothers telling their children, *biće bolje sine, biće bolje*. It will get better my child, it will get better. *Biće bolje* is fundamentally a refusal to give up hope, the last of the human freedoms. It is the practice of instilling in yourself and those around you the belief that, no matter how things are today, a better day will come. The secret in *biće bolje* is that the more you say it, the more you actually believe it and the more likely that you will recognise that better day when it arrives.

Apparently that day was here.

And I needed a man.

Even though I had hair and looked somewhat like the old me, psychologically it was a huge shift to move into the new body. I was still in mid-shift.

"You need a man to appreciate you, to make you feel like a woman again," reiterated Holly.

I thought about it. The idea of dating someone I had to start to get to know made me shudder. I could just picture it. There we would be over decaf, non-fat extra-hot lattes.

"Yeah, I just finished a stint in Singapore and I'm moving on to start my own consulting business. In my spare time I really enjoy golfing and the cottage. What do you do?"

"Well, I just finished a year of treatment for breast cancer."

At which point inevitably his eyes would dart down to my chest as his brain tried to remember where the Starbucks exits were located.

"Oh, I still have them, I just had a lumpectomy where they take out the cancer cells" or "Oh, and I don't know if I can have kids because the side effects of the chemo stopped my period and I'm waiting for it to come back but it hasn't yet" or "In my spare time I like getting checkups at Sunnybrook and saying hi to the radiation technicians I used to see every day. I really miss them since my treatment ended."

At this point, I couldn't bring myself to conjure up a resolution to this possible horrific date situation: a man had been the furthest thing from my mind. Unless, obviously, he was an oncologist, the only kind of man who could ever understand me again. But then who really wants to take their work home with them? As this verbal diarrhoea was being delivered over the phone to Holly, she in her ultimate wisdom, suggested a candidate.

His identity will remain under wraps. At university his nickname was the International Man of Mystery. He was a mutual friend of mine and Holly's from our university days. He and I had a bit of a crush on each other back then. Holly's suggestion was pure genius. Someone I already knew, a friend, and who was, according to Holly's most recent investigations, single. I thought about it. She told me to look him up and give him a call. I promised I would.

Because Holly, bless her heart, is an A-type personality real-estate lawyer and extremely efficient in closing a deal, she called me every day and asked if I had called him yet. Every day I answered in the negative.

I made excuses. I was busy. I was in court the next day.

Really I wasn't ever planning to call him. I was going to blow Holly off until she forgot about it or until she got tired of asking me. The more I thought about calling him, the more nervous it made me. First of all, how could he be single? He was successful and six foot two.

They're not usually single.

They have girlfriends or, at the very least, a cast of women trying out for the role. Although this would not usually have posed a problem for my only-child princess persona, my post-cancer mind was sure that he had several women and that, of course, they all had thick, long, shiny hair like I had when he saw me last. I was even surer that none of them had a scar on her left breast from an extremely cosmetically successful lumpectomy performed by the god of cancer surgeons, Dr. McCready. And it wasn't so much the hair and the scar on my breast that made me uncomfortable about meeting a man, even an old crush. My biggest insecurity was the scar of my experience that had left me raw and vulnerable and, I thought, unable to be normal again. Unable to have a conversation that didn't include the words "chemo", "breast" and "Bosnia". I'd been booted from a life in another country and thrown into a life in hospitals. I actually missed the hospitals when I finished treatment. I missed my doctors and the medical staff that I was used to seeing every day. Strangely enough, Sunnybrook had become my happy place, my comfort zone. As traumatic as my experiences had been, Sunnybrook was, outside of my life in Bosnia, all I knew. One day Holly finally broke.

"If you don't call him, I will."

I knew she would and I was more scared of her wrath than the possible outcome of the call I was about to make.

"You're back in town?"

"Ah, yeah," I answered.

The sound of the warm baritone voice suddenly made me nervous.

"Since when?"

"Um, well, it's been 18 months."

"What? And you're just calling me now?"

Here we go, everything came back to that. Holly had already coached me.

"Just tell him everything the first time you see him. That way, if he can't handle it, you didn't waste your time."

I loved Holly's rationality. Her advice was the perfect foil to my near-hysterical anxieties.

We agreed that he'd pick me up after work the next week and we'd go for lunch. Because I'd made such a fuss about calling him and spent hours on the phone asking Holly what I should say if he said this or asked that, Holly had kindly offered to come along so I could use the comfort of her presence as a way of getting over the big hurdle of having lunch alone with a man who was not an oncologist.

"Holly can come next time," was his curt response to my suggestion. I exhaled and began to psych myself up for the semi-date with the old law school crush who was expecting to see a girl with hair down to her waist and a steely will to save the world.

The old me.

The Street of Good Fortune

When he picked me up, he didn't look disappointed that my hair wasn't long like before. Like the old me. "I like your haircut," he said. "It brings out your eyes." It was the first time that I felt like I had a genuine encounter with someone who'd known the old me and had no idea that it was no longer her sitting next to him. I sensed appreciation and maybe some excitement. He was truly happy to see me and, in turn, his feelings for me rubbed off on me. After months of seeing myself through the eyes of doctors and nurses and technicians and devastated friends and family, I saw myself through his eyes and I wasn't sick or broken or less than whole. I was beautiful and desired and he liked my hair. The first two were unspoken sentiments that hung in the air like the thick, lovely smell of pine intermittently overpowered by lavender that defined summer evenings on outside terraces at the Croatian coast. A smell of happiness.

It was all too much. I couldn't do happy and light and falling in love. It wasn't reality. My brain yelled "cut" like an overzealous director who was never satisfied no matter how many different ways the actors repeated the take.

"I didn't cut my hair."

I stared at him, goading him, waiting to pounce on him with my cancer. Waiting to throw it at him and sit back to see what he did. Defending myself by expecting the worst, expecting him to recoil, to cut our lunch short and never call again. I was deathly afraid of rejection. I didn't realise I was afraid of this until moments before he picked me up when he called me and told me he was at the intersection where we'd agreed I'd be waiting.

"Did you just walk by?" he asked. "I saw a girl that looked just like you walk by."

I knew what he meant. He had just seen a girl with long hair and a bounce in her step walk by his car and thought it was me. It then suddenly occurred to me that I would disappoint him, that his law school crush would topple unceremoniously from her pedestal, that he'd wonder what he'd been thinking all that time ago when he'd drive me to the mall and patiently wait until I'd read the back of every new bestseller in the Chapters store, that the "princess" he jokingly used to call me would underwhelm him, fall short of his expectations, and he'd take refuge in the hordes of blonde groupies with long hair and perfect breasts that were vying for the passenger seat in his life.

I started to hyperventilate on my way out of the Shopper's Drug Mart in the underground mall where I was waiting for him and was suddenly overcome by a kind of fear I hadn't felt for a long time. The fear of exposing myself to the world of men, the world that I'd so deliberately excised from my universe that night before my first chemo when it became clear to me that my survival required such a move. The fear of being rejected at the time when I most needed acceptance and love. Like most debilitating fears, it was a fear born out of a feared event that had happened.

"What do you mean you didn't cut your hair?"

The Street of Good Fortune

He looked at me, slightly puzzled. At the table where we were sitting the September sun streamed through the half-open window and I looked at him and asked, "Why do you think I came back here?"

He was silent. "I'd really never have come back here unless I had to, unless it was a matter of life and death."

Then my favourite scene in this semi-date with an old law school crush whom I hadn't seen in years and never thought I would be seeing in this way, after my personal tsunami, as another me. He clasped his hands together on the table in front of him and leaned forward, which made his broad shoulders hunch a bit, and fixed his gaze on me and through me with a look in his eyes that was faintly, yet achingly, familiar. My fears and hesitations drowned in his look and I told him how sick I'd been and that I'd had a year of treatment that had culminated in eating kebobs with him. I think I squirmed more than usual. I do when I'm nervous and his only movement was to lean further towards me, sliding his hands, still clasped together, closer to me across the table and gazing through me with that look.

His next question gave away his future intentions.

"What do they look like now?"

He was asking about my breasts.

"I have a scar," I told him. "A big scar across my left breast."

"They look good from here. Besides, with the technology they have these days, it's probably barely noticeable."

At the end of the meal I wanted to see him again. I hadn't expected to feel this way and I didn't know what to do. The future, even next week, was something I'd stopped planning a long time ago. My only plans were to just feel better tomorrow than I did today. And it's what I told him when he asked me what I wanted from him. I looked into his face at our second dinner, a sombre event where I filled in the blanks of my recent history, about how my last relationship had ended, and that what I really wanted was for him "to just make me forget". It wasn't a request or an offer really, more just an articulation of the only kind of relationship I thought I was capable of.

He himself was a child of history. A history not unlike the history of the world for which I pined. A history of guns, tanks, trenches, loss and survival. An African history that he'd narrowly escaped. A history he rarely spoke about except in metaphors and veiled references. A history he'd overcome but still couldn't shake. A history that brought us closer and yet kept us apart. A history that had shaped him into a stoic, serious, perhaps even distant man on the outside while his interior remained intact. Vulnerable and often sweet. That second date he picked me up at work and we ended up at Boston Pizza, an establishment I only agreed to because it was close and he was hungry. He wore his barrister's gown, having rushed over from a trial, and he looked tired, edgy and actually quite sexy. Broad shoulders covered by a black gown loosened at the neck, topped by a face like thunder, the result of having been blasted by a crusty judge. He looked like some kind of legal superhero who needed a vacation. Something about the roughness in his look excited me. I hadn't been excited like that for a long time.

As though he'd been given an assignment he had to complete to the best of his ability, he began to make me forget.

I was the no-pressure girl. No dreams of buying houses or planning babies, I was happy to live for the moment. He called me every day religiously except Sunday, a religious exception I had to allow, and those days revolved around the moment when, usually between 10 and 11 am, my phone would vibrate to show his number on the screen. This became my wake-up call. I would sleep until his call, confident that it would happen as if I had set an alarm clock.

"Wake up, princess," his voice would glide through the phone and I would, only to spend the next hours primping myself for our lunch or dinner date. I took new interest in how I looked and started buying tight little dresses and patterned tights. I did my hair, something that took some new skills since it had grown back, not straight and thick like before but in a curly mop. I even started to like how I looked as I shaped the curls with gel, a never-before-seen product in my beauty repertoire.

"Your hair is so long now," he would say encouragingly every once in a while but mostly he didn't have to speak because, with him, I saw how he felt in his eyes. I wasn't used to being told secrets without hearing the words, the silence inherent in the communication making it all the more powerful in our dance of silent messages.

Sad and haunting, his eyes would settle on me as I jabbered on about something that had happened during my day and gesticulated animatedly with my hands and my voice until I suddenly realised that he'd been silent for some time. Since I was an only child and used to being the only voice I listened to, this realisation often took more than 10 or 15 minutes, when I'd stop and look at him sheepishly. It would be then that I would see that look. That look I remembered from a different time and place, a place of loss and hate and love and pain softened by tiny specks of tenderness directed at me. As if he realised it was somehow overwhelming, he would dim its intensity by slowly looking down so that his long eyelashes covered most of his dark, dark pupils and I would, as if on cue, go on with my story.

I painted pictures in my head. Pictures of us, of our mixed-marriage baby, a mix of his colour and mine. But this time, not like before, not like Bosnia, they were pictures of possibility. Not pictures of a life I'd painted but pictures of a life I never expected to want, a life in the world of my present. The world I'd waited so long to escape, the world I had escaped, and the world that had saved my life. The world in which I was biding my time until Dr. Verma gave me the all-clear to return to where I really wanted to be. Where I wanted to be was a mythical place, ever-changing in the annals of my mind, a sacred shining as it appeared in my mind's eye. A place I longed for and feared knowing that it was part real, part fable.

The Street of Good Fortune

Except that one day I just wanted to be in the world with him. Quietly it crept up on me, this feeling that I fought against and then didn't recognise and finally questioned over and over again as it slowly made itself a force to be reckoned with in my heart.

"I love you," I told him.

He smirked.

"For all the wrong reasons."

I didn't understand.

"My best friend warned me about this with you," he spat out bitterly. "Now you call me, Manteghi? Why didn't you bother to call me back then, when things were going well?"

He was referring to two summers before when I'd returned home for a visit and he called me to arrange a friendly lunch. I'd promised to call back and never had, busily passing the days until I could get back to the life I hung onto tightly for fear that it would somehow escape from me if my attention focused anywhere else even for a moment.

This he held against me.

Not the cancer or the scar but the fact that when I'd returned home for a visit before, as the old me, the me who had no idea what was around the corner, the me who thought she was on top of the world, the me who was no longer, I hadn't bothered to call him back. It became a wall that he erected between us whenever I asked more from him.

I couldn't understand this wedge between us. To me, it was either a manifestation of his highly fortified defence mechanism, or an excuse not to commit. Ironically, there was probably no other man I could have allowed into my life in the same way that I had him. True, it had been Holly's idea to call him. But had it not been him, my law-school personal trainer, friend and crush, someone I thought I could trust with my broken, raw, almost unrecognisable self, I would never have agreed. I tried to explain this to him but to no avail. Nothing I said could change his mind. I stopped trying. In our equilibrium, there were moments when I knew he was the man for me and that we'd be together as a family, cut short by moments when I was gripped with heart-racing fear that we would come to naught. That the end would be a future where he wouldn't come through, where he'd drop out right when I'd finally become comfortable believing that he would never leave.

"Where is this going?" I would ask him, afraid of letting myself be led down a path with no destination.

"I'm not going anywhere Manteghi, why are you trying to rush things?"

Rush things? Was he crazy? I'd just lost months and months to cancer, not to mention all the years before living a life that suddenly seemed not to count for very much. A life that had branded me as crazy and weird in the larger community and had culminated in frozen ovaries and an involuntary buzz cut.

After having been freed from the prison my body had become during the cancer and slowly recovering from my status as emotional refugee in a country where no one valued my life's most valuable currency, my experiences, perspective and thoughts, I had to make up for lost time. I had to catch up in this world that I'd now become a part of, even though I didn't have the slightest idea how this catching up was done in a free-market, non-post-conflict, consumer society. My friends told me as much.

"Has he taken you home?" asked Holly two months into our courtship.

"No," I replied, surprised at the question.

"Well, there's something wrong with that. He should take you home this Christmas. If he doesn't, stop seeing him. He's not serious. Don't waste your time."

Truthfully, I didn't know how to do domestic relationships. I didn't know what I should expect or what milestones should happen when. I knew only how to conduct myself in the standard Balkan-style relationship where Man-Boy and I spent most of our time together in the kind of routine where Sunday dinners with his grandmother and weekly phone calls to his sister were orchestrated by me. I would drink coffee with his friends' significant others while he went out with the boys and we were a couple as far as the *čaršija*, the general public, was concerned. *čaršija* was like "people" in "What will people say?" or "People's uprising". When I'd go to buy fruit at the local *granap*, the Bosnian equivalent of corner store, they would greet me with "*Evo ti ona, Jasminova*". Here she is, the one that belongs to Jasmin. Our couplehood was similar to most others around us. He would pick me up at work, driving being the man's responsibility in that world, and I learned how to make Turkish coffee and wash the floor on my hands and knees. No worthy Bosnian woman washed her floors with a mop. One day Man-Boy saw me mopping the kitchen floor and talking on the phone at the same time He looked displeased. "Meri, that will not get the floor clean. You have to use a rag on your hands and knees. Like this."

He was kind enough to show me.

I never questioned anything. I didn't wonder if he loved me or whether he'd propose. These were generally givens in the standard template of Bosnian relationships. Couples would date for some years and then, one day, there would be a wedding, a party with friends and family that was expected. I settled into my role as the woman in this holding pattern, confident in the predictability that such a relationship offered. It never occurred to me that my Man-Boy would lie or cheat and it never, ever occurred to me that he would leave me if I got sick. I would have sworn up and down that he'd be the first to offer his kidney if I needed it. The shock of his betrayal didn't hurt me as much as the marks it left.

The Street of Good Fortune

Having been conned by an ex who'd left me for dead, I was constantly on my guard, questioning everything and suspicious of his every move. When he didn't call me on Sundays, I wondered whom he was with and what he was doing. When his phone rang I'd immediately tense up, my imagination travelling to dark, terrible places almost in preparation for some inevitable dreaded event. He'd taken to announcing who was calling as though he could read my mind but the dread was stronger than me. It didn't help that he'd admitted he was still in contact with his ex who, according to him, wanted him back. I had no idea what that meant. Nothing good, I figured.

"I'm being honest with you, Manteghi."

I almost wished he wouldn't. I didn't know if I was allowed to ask or expect or even demand a different situation and I had no idea what to do to change my circumstances.

So it was only when grilled by Holly or other friends I went to for guidance that I found out what the relationship norms of my new world were. And IMM met few of them. He hadn't taken me home or out with his friends and he would decline any invitations from my curious and protective friends wanting the opportunity to impress upon him his responsibility to keep me unhurt and happy. The curious case of the ex that colonised my thoughts, no matter how consistent his attentions to me remained.

On one hand, he became the centre of my universe, the man I called whenever I was in distress, the man I could lean on and the man who supported my endeavours. On the other hand, his failure to engage in normal relationship activities kept me fearing that I was making the same mistake again. Investing my feelings in somebody who would one day rip the rug out from under my life, a new life built on sweat, tears, and eight rounds of chemo. I was convinced I would never recover from another blow.

I hated that I was so guarded, and had lost the ability to love without calculation. I lavished my affection only to frighten myself into retreat if he said the wrong thing, refused to mention plans, or didn't call me when he went home for Christmas holidays.

During my weeks or months of retreat, I'd curse the day I'd ever listened to Holly and agreed to call him. I consoled myself with the thought that whatever happened I always had Bosnia. I could always return to the country I loved and that loved me. I could never freeze him out for long, though, and sooner or later his place in my life would grow larger and deeper until it made more sense to have the real him in the flesh to love and to hate rather than the empty shell I talked to all day long in my head. He had graduated from alarm clock to my personal GPS. Whenever I was lost, a daily occurrence that I blamed on the short-term memory that chemo was known to erase, I'd call him, frantically trying to describe where I was and where I needed to be in exactly 15 minutes, a feat that could only be achieved if I were beamed to my destination.

"Manteghi, didn't I give you these directions yesterday?"

"OK, but I need them again, the chemo fried my brain, leave me alone, it's not my fault!" I'd whine.

He'd explain again how to exit at Eglinton Avenue and get back on the 401 at Kipling, bypassing the bottleneck. During our freezes, the weeks I refused to take his calls after he'd refused to take me somewhere or do something I considered necessary as proof of his honourable intentions, telling myself that it was over, that he didn't have it in him to commit, I'd magically remember all the shortcuts and directions he'd patiently directed me through and wistfully wish that he was back in my life. Our freezes always ended in a thaw of my making.

I'd look around at the couples in cafés and restaurants and in the circles of my acquaintance and wonder how they did it. How had they settled into this seemingly calm, idyllic couplehood that I was unable to attain? Unable even to figure out which steps theoretically led to this state of "normal". I studied these couples at every opportunity as they walked together in their own bubble of familiarity, without the sharp rises and falls that I seemed to share with him. It seemed effortless, but also one-dimensional. As bewitched as I was by their glossy public faces, I wondered what the reality was. I remembered how, at the height of my illness, in full chemo swing, my friend Sarah came to visit me every day. I couldn't understand how she could bear to look at me day after day, when I couldn't bear to look at myself, especially when she had a husband and a little girl at home. She persisted even after my parents asked her not to come by so frequently since, a mother of a three-year-old, she could harbour daycare germs that could prove fatal to me in my immune-depleted condition.

"Go home to your husband," my mother told her.

"It's OK. He's fine," she'd answer.

Once when my mother left the house and we were alone, me on the white wicker couch I inhabited and she in the chair beside me, thick, curly hair tumbling down her back, arrived at a family, a house, a job, not to mention her health, she got up to leave and said, "You know, don't think this is so bad. You'll get better but I'm stuck in this marriage".

Part of me felt I should be horrified that a friend should make such an insensitive statement, but I wasn't because I actually believed she felt that way. Her statement was so shocking and so genuine that I even felt a tiny sliver of relief that I was me instead of her.

So how had Christiane Amanpour ended up as Carrie in the most clichéd of *Sex and the City* relationships with her very own Big who wouldn't commit? When did the picture become more important than the reality?

At one point, when I felt better, much better, more like myself, my old self with some improvements, I stopped. I stopped wishing I was normal, not really even knowing what that meant. I stopped running after a picture I couldn't see myself in, a picture that was only a picture. I stopped running after things just because I didn't have them and others did, a trait that had never been one of my vices.

I had always been a dreamer and a rebel but Bosnia made me a fighter. And just in time. Bosnian women had discovered the holy grail of relationships. Well-versed in male imperfection, they were fighters, willing to wage war against high expectations and cookie-cutter couplehood for every scrap of happiness they could get. Moments they created for themselves and, through them, for those around them. They understood that under circumstances of imperfection, it's usually the woman's job to fight the hardest. Instead of railing against the unfairness of it, they took responsibility for their lives and the lives of those they loved. Uneven relationships but ones in which familiarity, habit and sacrifice built a life as stable as imperfection could permit. In a world rocked by war and ethnic cleansing, it was a given that men were fallible and that relationships, much like life, were impossible journeys interspersed with moments of joy that you looked back upon with bewilderment. They didn't expect happy endings or Vera Wang weddings with carefully colour-coded table coverings. They were the ultimate realists. This, in all its gritty, unpolished, ugly unfairness, was somehow comforting and inspiring. Making love the totality of moments ranging from exhilaration to devastation and back and forth until it became familiar, moments of gut-wrenching emotion tempered by silent Saturday morning coffees in cafés staring at *Dnevni Avaz* and *Oslobodjenje*, Bosnia's two biggest dailies. I always looked at those couples sitting face to face in cafés, without words, and felt their bond, built over years of tolerating moments of anger, betrayal and hurt, and sanded down at the edges with moments of lust, familiarity, habit and sacrifice which I understood as earned love, by not giving up.

I wanted to get up and scream at the women in my new/old world that so much of what they cared about didn't matter. That it didn't matter if he bought you a present on Valentine's Day or took you to the ballet. It didn't matter if he didn't want a couple's massage for his birthday or that he didn't tell you he loved you back every time you said it. What mattered was whether he'd take you to chemo and hold you when you looked like someone else, or something else. That only one real answer to the following question made a relationship: Was he there next to you when you needed him? And what was really scary was that you could never absolutely know the answer to this question until the worst happened. That was the crux of it all, that love was all about risk and fear and disappointment and faith and that it was often ugly but the parts between the ugly were worth it.

9

This Was the Man-Boy

Our first date took place in Tešanj, one of Bosnia's loveliest small towns. A little old Austro-Hungarian enclave filled with Ottoman-style mosques and stone houses interspersed with cafés, little restaurants and places where the bare mountain face framed by trees jutted out between buildings. We bought *čevape*, little beef kebabs in *somun* bread with diced onions and yoghurt and he led me up one of the green hills until we reached the top, where we sat down on the grass and ate our lunch beside the ruins of a fortress overlooking the minarets and rooftops of this magical little town, which could easily have been the scene of a fairy tale but was actually the place where my Man-Boy had spent his time in the army.

Tešanj had a warm, ethereal feel, like a little nest, and the whole town took on a cosy glow at dusk when all the lights in the houses and flats lit up the city, together making you feel like you were sitting at dinner with your family even when you were just sitting in a café alone. Eating my *čevape* on the hills overlooking a timeless, storybook place I felt like the princess bride; in love and inhabiting a slice of time in my own little reality where nothing else mattered, where physical and metaphysical laws didn't exist. Where the differences between us, Man-Boy and I, which in any other reality would have rendered our ill-fated union totally dysfunctional, seemed to dissolve into the clouds of fantasy and denial in my head.

I met Man-Boy for the first time at the Home and Families where I, with my rudimentary Bosnian, minus Alma — with whom I'd recently had a spat — was desperately in need of a language liaison. I was standing on the first floor of the building and he appeared from one of the rooms he knew so well, having grown up there. He came over, introduced himself, and his face in that moment is fixed in my mind, a moment that changed my course in more ways than I could have fathomed at the time. It was the face of someone who wouldn't hurt a fly. The face of a man with the expression of a wounded boy framed by a head of slightly greying hair that evoked in me a mix of feelings: twinges of pity and sympathy laced with a desire to protect, adding up to a wrench of the heart. A face that humanised my sense of mission, shaping it into a living person instead of the restless longing I'd felt as long as I could remember. Man-Boy was well aware of this singular quality he possessed, telling me later how, during the war, foreign journalists eager to evoke this exact feeling in their viewing public would come to the orphanage and ask to interview him, the little boy with the face. He gave interview after tearful interview until one day he refused to come down from his room when they asked for him. He didn't know why, he said when I asked, *samo tako*, just because.

Much, much later I wondered if I, too, had simply been another foreigner to whom he'd agreed to give an interview. For a price.

But not back then.

Back then, such thoughts were alien to me. At our first meeting his face invited me into hidden worlds to which he held the key. I followed eagerly, entranced by the places he led me, each one being a step deeper into the metamorphosis that I sought, transforming me from a foreign girl from Oakville with faded Iranian roots into one of them. He introduced me to his friends and translated not just people's words but their intentions. One day when we were walking by the orphanage, we passed one of the educators, a particularly slimy man with a revolting smile that made my stomach turn whenever I saw it directed at any of the children. He smiled as Man-Boy greeted him and asked him a question. It seemed like a pleasant exchange and I thought I'd perhaps been wrong about this man.

"Do you know what he asked me, Meri?"

I did not.

"*Jesi li je odradio?*" Have you done her yet?

I was appalled.

"What did you say?" I asked, wondering how this exchange had looked so innocent from the outside.

"I told him to fear Allah, Meri, just to fear Allah."

His integrity impressed me. Like many Bosnians of his age, he'd rejected the Communist values of his father's generation, which he believed had led the country into war. He sought refuge in religion. His religion of choice, or perhaps lack of choice, was Islam. Zenica was predominantly Muslim, having been the hub for thousands of Muslim refugees fleeing from ethnic cleansing in Central Bosnia, and the kids at the orphanage had been given religious instruction during the war by Imams and others with intentions I couldn't clearly grasp. What impressed me, though, was his discipline of praying several times a day as well as the marked difference I saw between him and the generation of educators who were his role models, shockingly unscrupulous and self-serving. Man-Boy's voluntary adherence to the tenets of his religion, albeit a narrow post-war version of it that often alarmed me, made me admire him.

What really left me defenceless where it came to him was how he was with the children. I met him as he was leaving one room or "family" of kids who ran after him grabbing his pant legs and calling out his name. He replaced Alma as my translator. I was bewitched by the way he sat with the children, gently talking to them and smiling at them with that face. I knew he had very little money but he'd sometimes put his hand in his pocket and hand one of the kids 50 Bosnian cents, or even a whole shiny silver KM, a mark, to buy an ice cream or a lollipop.

Later on when we were a couple and he drove a car, I'd visit the kids alone while he went out with his friends. "You visit the kids, Meri, and I'll pick you up when I'm done." When he'd arrive he'd send one of the kids playing outside to get me, preferring to wait for me in the car, a shiny black Fiat bought with the same quality that attracted foreign journalists and foreign girls, smoking and laughing with his friends. How could I hold this against him? I understood. He'd had enough of the orphanage to last him a lifetime. The children asked for him every time; I told them he had obligations, "*Imao neka obaveza*", a convenient little phrase that in Bosnian sounds serious but could mean anything. A phrase that encompassed a myriad of possibilities for his not showing up, a chic veil of a phrase behind which you could hide if you had no real excuse.

Man-Boy became my constant companion while I was in Zenica at the orphanage, which was almost every day. Through him, I gained total access to this place, which had been like a fortress to me. I walked in and out of the children's rooms freely and sometimes even at the invitation of the educator, who would make us Turkish coffee. We'd sit in her room and discuss the children, the other educators, and generally end in discussing her personal problems. After each visit, Man-Boy would comment on what I'd heard and give me the uncensored, inside story about the origins of many of the children and how they had ended up at Home and Families. He told me stories of the educators and which ones were thieves. The biggest thief was the Director, Aida, the woman who'd kicked Man-Boy out of the orphanage when he was 14 in the middle of the war, and who also stole his and his siblings' monthly pensions, inherited from their father, over the years they were under her care. When, after his expulsion from the orphanage, Man-Boy went to his father's company to ask for the 10 years' worth of insurance money the company was responsible to pay out to him, the accountant was puzzled. She showed him the book of accounts proving that money had been faithfully paid out, month after month since his father's death, pages and pages of accounting ledgers that showed Director Aida's signature beside the monthly amount due to their dead employee's minor children.

My Man-Boy would point her out to me as we walked through the city on one of our many treks to buy a VCR for the children, or to take the smaller ones for ice cream. He'd smile at her calmly while I tried to glare across the road and curse her in my head as she walked across the street.

"Tell her she's a thief!" I would prod him,

"*Pusti sad to Meri, nije vrijedna moji riječi.,*" Forget that all now, Meri, she's not worth it.

I was in awe of his forbearance. I was incensed for him, for his brother and sister, for all the children who were being exploited and exposed to such monsters without the love and protection of their parents. The restless longing inside me found a home at the orphanage. It was like I'd been waiting for this mission since I could remember and it had come to me. I couldn't have articulated what it was exactly, but I did undertake, without realising it at the time, to take on what they felt and to feel with them, and in so doing to rebalance the universal scales of justice. How it would help them I didn't know. Perhaps I thought that by their knowing somebody cared, that somebody was willing to suffer with them, to empathise, it would help, I would help, and they would be saved.

What would happen to me never crossed my mind. In my man-boy's mentality, my future, my life, and my well-being were givens in this world. No matter how hard I tried, when push came to shove, I was a foreigner and I would always be OK. He didn't have to say it. I just knew.

He told me in the way he asked me for money to give to his friends, even though he knew my contract would end in a month. He told me every time he'd lend our car to whoever asked, no matter how irresponsible or drunk, saying that it was expected of him, just like it was expected of me to put my needs aside. He told me when he spent more and more time without me, drinking with his friends, or randomly quit the jobs I found him. He told me when he racked up expenses I had to pay when he knew I was rifling through my contacts, calling all the organisations that had ever been in Bosnia, desperately looking for a job.

And while Man-Boy was my ticket to Bosnianness, I never quite made his inner circle. A girl who could never know how he'd suffered, who could never understand him, and who'd never experienced the ravages of the kind of life he had lived. A girl who should only give, having been so blessed with the fickle advantages of parents and geography.

I didn't see it then though. Not when he looked at me with that face, the face that had launched my sense of mission.

We ate together in Zenica's fast-food places and Café Tropik, where they served *produžena sa šlagom*, espresso with real whipped cream, my new favourite drink. We ate at Café Dallas, on the densely green outskirts of the city when I had the car, the little red hatchback VW whose gears I joyfully abused, filled with a strange, wild feeling of freedom as I drove through the country. I pulled down on the stick shift to speed the little car into fourth gear then up to fifth like my life depended on it, filled with a sense of exhilaration I couldn't explain, but revelled in. Later on when Man-Boy moved to Sarajevo to be closer to me and to the job I'd found for him selling Persian carpets he taught me things outside the orphanage. Like how to say *ljubav*, love and *prijateljica*, friend, helping me to pronounce the almost impossible sound that the letter *lj* makes in Bosnian. We'd go back to Zenica, or drive to Mostar, halfway to the Croatian coast, one of the most beautiful cities in the Balkans, and he'd turn up the radio and teach me everything I needed to know to be Bosnian. Through him, I learned to recognise Bosnia's iconic singers, loved and revered by all ethnic groups equally, music being the transcendental space of national unity. We listened to Zdravko Čolić 's singular ballads and Kemal Monteno's warm, smooth voice that evoked in me fatalistic, melancholic longing.

One Sunday a month Man-Boy and I had dinner at his grandmother's house. I loved Baka the first day I met her. Although she was not particularly religious, did not display a cross in her home, and spoke wistfully about *Titova Država,* Tito's state, she did not approve of the new postwar extremist Islam that her grandsons had adopted. She was in her seventies, and spoke only Bosnian. She had made one trip to Australia to visit her brother, but had suffered such severe nausea on the plane that she vowed never to travel again.

On our first meeting she opened the door to her tiny flat in the Blatuša section of Zenica and I saw a tall, slim, poised woman with white hair and beautiful hands. She kissed my Man-Boy and his brother three times, the only obvious sign of her Serb ethnicity. As they walked into her flat, she fixed her eyes on me. They told me that she was a woman who'd been orphaned as a child and survived two wars, told me that she'd lost her only daughter, my Man-Boy's mother, first to a violent marriage and finally to a terrible disease that left her three orphaned grandchildren. They told me that she could tell who was good and who wasn't. I knew she was looking into my soul to determine just that. Then I saw a softness cross her face, a look that always greeted me whenever I saw her. By hand she made me *burek,* filo pastry filled with minced meat, a dish I only ate at her house.

"*Nemoj po gradu jesti burek Meri, Boga pitaj od čega im je mesa.*" Don't eat *burek* in town, Meri; God only knows where their meat comes from.

So I didn't. Baka was an exceptional cook and made Turkish coffee strong enough to pass for a prohibited substance if you happened to drink it before Olympic drug testing. In the beginning my Man-Boy would drink my coffee as well as his own while Baka's back was turned so she wouldn't get offended. Later on, when my stomach became Bosnian, Baka made coffee once before and once after dinner especially for me. She invited us for *iftar*, the breaking of the fast once every Ramadan, the Muslim month of fasting, out of respect for her grandsons, when she cooked a huge feast, an incredible feat on such a tiny pension.

She knew that I was not Muslim and asked me when my holiday was so she could make me a feast on that day, too. She asked about my religion with genuine curiosity and I struggled with explaining theological concepts in Bosnian.

When I finished, she concluded, with a knowing look at Man-Boy, "*Znači ko ne poštuje tudje ne poštuje ni svoje,*" meaning he who doesn't respect other faiths doesn't respect his own either. I later realised that Baka was the first Bosnian human rights activist I ever met.

While Baka's was a close second, no one made Turkish coffee like my Seka, the sister I claimed through belonging to my Man-Boy. She consistently achieved the thickest layer of *kajmak*, the foam on top of the coffee that measured the skill of its maker. Seka and her family lived in Republika Srpska, better known as the RS. Since the end of the war, Bosnia was divided into two entities, a genius move masterminded by the last set of international ambassadors sent to a then-warring but still united Bosnia and Herzegovina over a four-year period to politely negotiate with bloodthirsty war criminals about whether they would like — when they weren't elbow-deep in genocide of course — to end the war. The RS was the other side of the country, with its own corrupt government, head of government and ministers that, along with the Federation side,

The Street of Good Fortune

sucked Bosnia dry of any possibility of prosperity, economic or otherwise, for the people they allegedly represented.

My Seka, her husband and their three children were some of those lucky participants in the nation's march toward Western democracy, a concept which ensured that the same leaders who had led the country into war were recycled, wrapped in new and improved nationalist identities, and drove the country further into disaster while enriching themselves and their families, parading around the country with shiny luxury vehicles and bad haircuts.

Seka lived in Posavina, the only famously flat stretch of Bosnia and Herzegovina's hilly landscape. Her little farmhouse was surrounded by cornfields and her front yard was inhabited by chickens and at least one rooster, whose presence was always signalled at about 5:30 every morning, the noise blasting through the tiny orange ear-plugs I always inserted before bed. Seka herself woke up at this time, having become a country girl since her marriage to her first husband, a Serb from the mountains, where she moved to live with him and his family soon after her eighteenth birthday.

"*Meri, ništa nisam znala kad sam se udala, sve sam poslije naučila.*" Meri, I didn't know how to do anything until I got married, she consoled me when my Man-Boy complained of my lack of domestic skills.

"Look at Seka," he would say as he watched her work busily in her makeshift kitchen that, despite its very basic appliances and lacking a counter or a sink, was spotless at all times.

"My sister cooks and cleans all day long for five people without running water," he boasted from his chair, one leg crossed over the other, his elbow perched on the chair's armrest, his head surrounded by a halo of smoke from the cigarette in his hand. It wasn't the custom for him to help in the kitchen. Bosnian men rarely did and Seka would never expect it.

I, however, offered, "*Seko, daj mi nešto da radim*". Seka, give me something to do. She sometimes would. She'd ask me to slice tomatoes or cucumbers, easy, happy tasks to make me feel included, tasks that took me twice the time it would have taken her. I'd slice a tomato while Seka made bread, something she did every day.

"Why does Seka make her own bread?" I asked my Man-Boy on that first trip. It was such a long, painstaking process, requiring real physical strength to knead the dough into submission then shape it into a loaf. I asked her to let me try, thinking it looked so fun, all this kneading. Several seconds after a cramp disabled my hand and I cried out, she smiled, took the plastic bowl away from me and poured me a Turkish coffee before continuing her task.

A loaf of bread only cost one mark or about 70 cents. I knew this even though I rarely bought bread from the bakery, preferring the imported Swiss pumpernickel loaf I found at the gourmet deli on Sarajevo's Ferhadija Street.

"Meri, they'd need to buy three loaves a day and they can't afford to spend three KM a day just on bread."

I felt ashamed for asking. Despite living in Bosnia for some time, the realities of the country, the life most people struggled with daily always managed to surprise me. Bosnians are a proud people. Although their war exposed them to the glare and not-so- good intentions of the world, they hid their personal struggles with such aplomb that even to the semi-trained eye they were invisible. Not being a complete foreigner I could tell that Seka was poor. She lived in temporary housing, having fled her home village during the war when Muslim forces drove everybody out.

But in my mind, the word poor didn't apply to Seka, not the one I visited, the one who cooked three hot meals a day for us, who had a never-ending supply of sweet coffee, which I drank in quantities that surprised even the locals. Not the one who called me before our departure from Sarajevo to ask what pastry I liked, which she made, a sweet, frothy dessert called *šampita*. Not the Seka who consoled and befriended me, taking my side in my arguments with her brother, telling me to leave him when things got bad, when his demanding nature and irresponsibility drove me to call her.

"Meri, don't put up with this. You'll find somebody else in Canada and you'll always be welcome in my home."

At Seka's I felt rich. As an only child, I'd always wondered how it felt to have siblings, craving that closeness and intimacy with someone who had grown up with me. During my childhood, when my parents would fight, and later after they divorced, I always wished I'd had a sister, someone who would understand how I felt; someone who was on my side. I'd felt alone for so long in my own little world of one. Seka did not just welcome me into her family; she wove me into its makeup in a million tiny ways. She'd lower her voice sometimes and talk to me in a "females only" tone about her kids, and give me relationship advice.

"You're too nice to him, Meri, don't be so nice, he'll get out of hand."

She asked for my picture and put it inside a frame with the picture of my Man-Boy, half covering his face. She told me how to cook *grah*, beans Bosnian style, over the phone and which teas I should take for whatever ailment I had. When I called her to tell her I was going to see the doctor to check a lump in my breast, she asked me where her brother was.

"Meri, come here, we'll take you to the doctors we know. And he's doing God knows what in Zenica letting you go to the doctor alone!" she muttered in disgust.

"It's not another girl, it's just that this between us isn't going to work..." He trailed off.

I hung up.

So ended my five-year relationship with my Bosnian orphan.

The Street of Good Fortune

The night before I was to start chemotherapy.

I sat down on the toilet seat and thought, this is it. I've hit rock-bottom. I felt stabbed in the heart with a molten-hot knife. At the same time, I felt that an immense weight was lifted from me. Two equal yet completely opposite emotions that technically should have cancelled each other out so that I would just feel nothing.

I'd been in the bathroom so that nobody could hear my conversation. Speaking "that language" in my house had become more and more difficult. As far as my parents were concerned, Bosnia might just as well have been called "the country that gave my daughter cancer"; anything originating from there was non-grata. This was uncomfortable not only because I, the me who returned, had come from there, and also because everything that made me feel in any way better, that comforted me, made me happy or helped me cope, came from there. In fact, I was a stranger now to my own country and to my own family. They didn't understand me and I railed against my return to a place I thought I would never again call home.

After Man-Boy and I spoke on the phone, I didn't have an epiphany. It was just my voice of reason, suddenly freed from heavy denial and illusion that had kept it down for so long. I began to put sentences together in my head to make sense of the last 15 minutes of my life.

"After everything you did for him…"

I hated that sentence at once but there it was and I had no more denial left to hide it behind.

"After everything you went through together…"

This sentence was more palatable. After everything we'd been through together I couldn't believe, couldn't accept, that during the most horrible moment of my life, he'd simply dismissed our relationship with "It's not what you think. It's not another girl". I wouldn't have thought it was another girl. Not until he said it anyway. Not that I didn't think there were probably other girls while I had been in Canada being diagnosed with cancer. Nothing serious, probably some flirting and dancing and maybe more. But I wouldn't have ever thought that was the reason that he ended it.

No.

Because my voice of reason, recently liberated from a five-year slumber, told me: "He's a spineless coward. Don't hate him." And I didn't. Not then, anyway. But while I didn't hate him, I couldn't accept the fact. The fact that mattered was that, during my time of need, he left me for dead. He didn't ask how I was, didn't call any of my friends to inquire about me and, worst of all, he let his family, the family I loved, believe that I'd left him and Bosnia to go "back to my mother", like a spoiled foreigner who'd had some kind of Balkan jungle fever and decided it was time to go back to the good life. Like the exact kind of person I could never be. In the blink of an eye, he reversed the metamorphosis, the gift he'd given me of his world, taking it back when it was all I had left.

The Street of Good Fortune

Since my plan had always been to return to Sarajevo, I'd travelled home with a small suitcase and very few belongings. Everything else remained untouched in a quaint little flat across from the *Narodna Banka*, the National Bank, in a courtyard beside Café Imperijal, the only one of Sarajevo's cafés that proudly displayed a Christmas tree in its window every December and served Turkish coffee generally only available in homes and the coffeehouses of the Old Town. Despite the very slight smell of sewage that greeted you at the door when you entered, Café Imperijal welcomed me on the mornings I would roll out of bed and immediately require a strong Turkish coffee before becoming fully human. Clearly though Turkish coffees at the Imperijal were a thing of the past and my flat needed to be cleaned out and returned. This I had counted on my Man-Boy to do, the now sole driver of our car. When my friend Lejla called me to tell me he refused to even discuss helping with the move I stopped breathing for a minute with the shock of it. I'd been erased. I no longer mattered, no longer had use.

Tammy was my main chemo nurse. She was in charge of the patients being treated in clinical trials. She was, as far as I could tell, around my age and sported a perky blond ponytail and big baby blue eyes rimmed with black mascara-laden eyelashes. She had a healthy, happy, clean look and I liked her smile. She was part cheerleader, part scientist, and my father's personal favourite.

In a good way.

"That girl has a good head on her shoulders," he said of her, a huge compliment coming from him. She was the white, blonde, small-town foil to Dr. Verma's cosmopolitan Bollywoodness. When I complained about losing my hair, she told me about her friend with alopecia, a condition of permanent baldness. When I asked her if she thought my period would come back, she reminded me that even at 34, without the chemo and without a husband, my chances of getting pregnant were not great so not to worry about that. She was straight up, didn't sugarcoat, but was positive and the only person I trusted to tell me the truth. I complained about the fertility clinic and how I'd felt like a woman in *The Handmaid's Tale* and she cringed and wrote something down on her clipboard. The more I saw of her the more I liked her. She always had time for me.

During one of my appointments so Tammy could inject me with a very expensive, luxury potion that triggered my white blood cells to keep multiplying despite the shock of the chemo cocktail, she asked, "Is your boyfriend coming from Bosnia?"

That's how it started, how I told Tammy that my Man-Boy had broken up with me the night before my first chemo and that I hadn't heard from him since. She looked up at me with an initial look of distress that in a moment turned into matter-of-fact.

"It's very common," she said.

The Iranian in me waited for some wailing and at least five minutes of pity, an emotion I'd feel victorious to evoke in her. She remained matter-of-fact and told me that boyfriends, husbands, and husbands who are also fathers, often deserted women with breast cancer. She once had a patient whose husband had left her and their three children in the middle of her treatment.

"It's hard for them too," said Tammy. "They feel so powerless, so out of control."

I liked Tammy but I gave her a look inherited from my mother and Balkanised. When she stuck the needle in my arm I barely felt it.

Months later, when I'd almost finished radiation I got a Facebook message from the Man-Boy who'd left me for dead almost a year before.

"How are you? I think about you sometimes and how you are. This time has been really hard for me."

I couldn't believe what I was reading. I thought I'd made a mistake and went back to read it again. Had I not been bombarded with pictures of him clutching at various girls during a New Year's celebration right before reading his message, I might have thought that in his one-room flat in Zenica he was repentant, depressed, and haunted by the evil of his ways. Had I not received news of his escapades, sightings of him driving around the city with girls perched on the back of his brand-new motorcycle, I might have thought he'd been gripped by such sadness that he'd been unable to speak of me without falling apart.

For some time I felt nothing for him. When he was mentioned, I was unmoved. In my desire to preserve the sacred memories of my life in Bosnia, I carefully excised him from the pictures in my mind, someone without whom so many of my beloved experiences could not have been possible, reducing him to a grey background shadow. But as time passed and I was forced to face my demons, the demons that stood between me and my happiness in the world responsible for my survival, I forced myself to feel for him. Forced myself to open and clean out the last closet of my pre-cancer life to make room for the feelings waiting for me in a future only I had the power to determine.

As I did, I realised that I had one last, pressing, urgent wish for him. A desire that increased in passion as the time approached for my long-awaited return trip to the home of my rise and fall, and of the memories that had sustained me through this journey I often didn't want to believe was mine. This last wish was to return tanned, triumphant, with beautiful, long hair flowing in the wind, cleavage prominently displayed, stand on the cobblestones of my beloved Čaršija in front of the Begova mosque, and come face to face with him. Face to face with that look that had so tricked me about its bearer those years ago and to slap that lie as hard as I could; hard enough to leave a scar so deep and ugly that it would remind him of me whenever he looked in the mirror. Remind him of the days I spent watching a red poison burn through my veins to save my life. Remind him of the burns on my newly stitched breast that the nurse dressed with bandages every day as beads of sweat dripped down my face from the pain. Remind him of the days I'd sit in hospital after hospital waiting for answers to questions I never thought I'd be asking. Remind him of the day Dr. Verma gave me the news that my past had irrevocably changed the course of my future. I daydreamed about this wish without shame, without remorse, and with relish. Yet although many long-awaited events are much sweeter in anticipation than culmination, I knew in my heart this wasn't one of them.

10

An Iranian in Bosnia

When I first walked down the Kovači Tapetar hill towards Sebilj, Sarajevo's Pigeon Square, I wondered where I was. What strange place was this that hovered between the present and the past, reality and fantasy? I took in the scene of mosques, the covered women below me, and the sound of the call to prayer. My reaction was fear. Having grown up with a well-founded fear of all things Islamic derived from fleeing a revolution in which Baha'is were brutally persecuted, the sight of *hijabs*, *niqabs*, and bearded men with rolled-up pant legs was not a scene I welcomed in a European capital. Would they realise that I was a Baha'i and come after me?

I looked around for a store that appeared to belong to the present and found a tiny fake designer perfume shop with a very blonde employee who was sufficiently underclothed to merit my confidence. I entered the shop, leaned over to her and whispered, "Where can I go where people look normal?"

She chuckled and directed me out of Pigeon Square and down to Ferhadija Street, where girls in short-shorts and high-heeled sandals kissed their clean-shaven and heavily gelled boyfriends in cafés serving beer and pizza. I sighed in relief and continued exploring this unreal city that was a maze of contrasts, contradictions and extremes co-existing in a natural way no one seemed to question.

People did, however, question me. "You're from Iran?" they asked when I revealed my origins. I had started out saying I was Canadian but when they heard my name they assumed I was part of their diaspora pretending to be foreign, which drew looks of disdain: "*Uf...jesi ufurana čovjeće!*" Wow, you're so conceited. So I went on to explain that I'd been born in Iran. Their eyes widened with a look of apprehension. "Why do you hit yourselves?" they'd ask me, their eyes filled with wonder. "Hit ourselves?" I had no idea what they were talking about.

It took me a while to figure out that they were referring to the Shiite holy day of Ashura, when the vexatious religious elements of Iranian society paraded through the streets and in fact did strike themselves, often until they bled, some using chains and sharp instruments to prove their dedication to Imam Hossein. According to my grandmother, a devout Shiite who did not hit herself, they hit other people, too, including religious minorities or *kafirs,* most of whom wisely preferred to stay indoors and draw their curtains on that particular day. I'm positive Imam Hossein himself would have been horrified at how this layer of the populace celebrated his memory. But then he'd been murdered almost a thousand years ago, without having had the chance to forbid such internationally embarrassing behaviour from his followers. It was left to me to explain that I did not hit myself — even when I felt like kicking myself – and not being a Shiite, couldn't logically explain why some of my fellow Iranians did. Almost half of Bosnia's population was considered Muslim according to statistics compiled by somebody and published as truth. But these were of the Sunni variety, spared from hitting themselves by the schism that divided Islam into two conflicting groups almost 1,400 years ago.

As an Iranian Baha'i forced out of my country by a revolution known as "Islamic", my relationship with Islam growing up had been tenuous. My father's mother had been a religious Shiite who'd prayed regularly and had even fashioned a tiny *chador* for me, a black covering like a cloak that I proudly wrapped around my five-year-old self when she donned her own larger one, and watched her pray. Before praying, I would follow her to the bathroom where she would perform *voozoo*, the obligatory washing of her hands and face before *namaz*, the obligatory prayer. Once she'd washed her hands and face she'd wash mine, scrubbing my little hands thoroughly. "You must be clean before you pray to God," she'd say. Then she would carefully unwrap from its velvet cover the stone upon which Shiite Muslims bow their foreheads during the *namaz* and proceed to pray in the living room. I liked our little ritual, and even though I attended Baha'i children's classes where boys and girls sat together and prayed in Farsi without covering, I instinctively respected my grandmother's obligatory prayer and sat quietly while she whispered in Arabic. On the wall above her there was a picture of the

Shah, Iran's self-proclaimed King of Kings, and his family. The Shah's reign came to an abrupt end in 1979 when he and his family fled the country with a chunk of its wealth in a private jet, leaving the nation to a herd of bearded butchers with an appetite for human flesh. The bloodbath that ensued in the country of my birth shaped much of my informal education about Islam.

My formal introduction to Islam came through Sarajevo's iconic *Islamski Fakultet,* Islamic Faculty, where my friend Dina and I registered for their six-month course on Islam, an English-language night course taught by the Faculty's *crème de la crème* for foreigners unfamiliar with Bosnian Islam —or any Islam. This was also a great opportunity for various Western embassies to send some of their less illustrious staff members to monitor this highly sensitive hub of underground *jihad*. Every Thursday at dusk Dina and I would walk up the gently sloped hill that led from Pigeon Square and enter the building through a majestic archway studded with tiny, geometric mosaics in warm yellows and oranges that led into a structure built around an open-air pool, the heart of the building, surrounded by marble pillars holding up the two storeys of classrooms and offices. I loved Thursday night class. I loved the sight of the Faculty at dusk set against the backdrop of Sarajevo's Old Town, above which minarets and trees stencilled the skyline in the shadow of the setting sun.

Professor Rešid Hafizović wore a black beret and looked like an artist you'd find in Paris of the 1950s sitting in front of an easel in Montmartre. He was an exceptional mind and the Faculty's specialist on comparative religion and on Shiite

Islam. Everything about him was civilised, refined, unassuming and gentle and he somehow hovered above everyone and everything else in the Faculty. His lectures were intellectually demanding and required an understanding of the metaphysical. Once, totally absorbed by his lecture on angels, which he'd begun by describing the characteristics of Izrail, the Angel of Death, my trance was interrupted by an American apparatchik who, along with the rest of her group, sat in the back like high school kids and was obviously not there because of an affinity for the metaphysical. "Um, do you mean like ghosts?" she asked with a slightly sarcastic inflection at the end of her sentence. I think she pictured Casper's unfriendly twin. Professor Hafizović, stunned by this question, remained silent for a moment but then said, "No, I mean angels".

Dina, my Iranian-born, Berkeley-educated friend, rolled her eyes. "Republicans," she muttered, "even their spies are dumb."

My favourite part of class, though, was the evening break when we filed downstairs to the basement cafeteria and mingled with the professors drinking Turkish coffee with sugar cubes. Iranians also drink their strong, black tea with sugar cubes, sucking on them to sweeten the tea that seeps through the cube, dissolving it in carefully timed stages until both tea and cube disappear together. This small ritual at every break gave me a wistful feeling of nostalgia for something or somewhere I could only faintly remember.

As a small child in Iran, I'd felt adored and loved as the youngest member of a large family in which there was a place that belonged just to me. In Canada, I'd look through the few albums we'd managed to save from Iran and gaze at the pictures of innumerable aunts, uncles and cousins, pictures in which I could detect a now-elusive feeling of warmth and love trapped in scenes that always caused my heart to tighten with a sense of overwhelming loss for a world full of emotion and depth I knew I could never feel in the bright new world of immigration. Pictures of my grandparents, my grandmother in a navy-blue silk dress and a string of pearls, and my grandfather in a three-piece suit and silver cufflinks. Pictures of me as a baby, in my room filled with stuffed animals, balloons, and white and pink furniture. Pictures of me in little MotherCare outfits that my mother would carefully select for me on our European vacations to visit relatives or attend a Baha'i conference. One of my favourite pictures was a black-and-white shot taken of my parents right before a night on the town. My mother is wearing a very short cream mini-dress and is six months pregnant with me. She is standing in front of my grandparents' staircase with one foot resting on the bottom step, gazing at the camera with a shy smile. She is wearing cream patent low-heeled pumps and has her hand in the crook of my father's elbow. My father is dressed in a hip, black suit with tapered pant legs, and has a moustache and a Beatles haircut. He is a newly-minted architect working in Tehran's most prestigious architectural firm responsible for the Shahyad, the monument that graces Tehran's main square and remains the backdrop for any official picture of the city. My mother is expecting me, unexpectedly, and finishing her studies in English literature at one of Tehran's private universities. It's a picture full of youth, hope, promise and love. They look like a happy couple with a bright future in a country on its way to democracy, prosperity and a new measure of stability. It's a picture of a life they never got the chance to live, a life suddenly darkened by the cloud of revolution forming overhead, unloosing a torrential downpour, the opposite of everything this picture represented.

Two of Sarajevo's swankiest buildings housed the embassy of the Islamic Republic of Iran and an Iranian Cultural Centre that was never open and conspicuously empty despite its central location on the city's busiest pedestrian thoroughfare. During the ethnic cleansing that took place in Bosnia, the Bosnian Army was hit with an arms embargo dictated by the UN Security Council while the two armies attacking it had divided the store of weapons held by the ex-Yugoslav National Army, at the time said to be the fourth largest army in the world. Contravening the embargo, the Iranian government had sent arms to the beleaguered Bosnian Army. This had bought them prime post-war Sarajevo real estate as well as the respect of many of Sarajevo's residents who'd felt, as snipers targeted their children and shells rained down upon their homes, that perhaps an arms embargo was not much of a solution.

Being Iranian in Bosnia gained me respect and set me apart from the other foreigners whose intentions were suspect for people who'd survived a war in which all things UN had left a bad taste in their mouths. The fall of Srebrenica, Bosnia's last safe haven during the war, where thousands of Muslim men and boys were murdered over a period of several days while a Dutch regiment of peacekeepers stood helplessly by, was the UN's biggest failure in international peacekeeping to date. Most Bosnians viewed any international efforts from then on through a thick filter of scepticism. It was a love-hate relationship, since many Bosnians were employed by international organisations paying salaries much higher than in local enterprises, allowing them to support their extended families in a country where pensions didn't even cover the cost of heating during Bosnia's harsh winters.

When I arrived in villages I visited working with the UNHCR, I was always introduced as "*Meri, naša Iranka*". This is Meri, our Iranian girl. A sudden change came over the people I met and their faces opened up. "*OOOh Iranka, to se slavi!*" Ooh, an Iranian girl! That calls for a celebration! In one village, the men who met us in front of the newly rebuilt mosque shook my hand vigorously, looked me up and down, and smiled at each other knowingly. "Our Imam needs a wife — you are perfect." Automatically my mind conjured up a picture of an old, fat, bearded Iranian mullah seeking a third wife. Before I could protest I was being led towards the mosque from which emerged a young, extremely handsome man with Hugh Grant hair wearing a chocolate suit that set off his tall, muscular frame. I suddenly felt that rollercoaster feeling in my stomach and my legs turned to jelly. "*This* is our Imam," declared one of the men victoriously. "This is our Iranka," he told the Imam, whose wide smile and strong hands already had me contemplating an afternoon wedding in the mosque behind him.

"I'm actually from Sarajevo, from Stup," he told me, mentioning a city neighbourhood. "I just come here for Fridays and holidays because they don't have a local Imam. We should go for coffee sometime." He smiled at me. My driver Nino snapped pictures of us and during the days and months that followed I often looked at pictures of my Imam that got away and wondered if I could have lived a happy Bosnian life as the exotic Iranian wife of the local Muslim cleric.

The fact that I could even speculate about such a thing was pure *Balkanika*, a term that referred to any phenomenon that was unique to the Balkans and unbelievable anywhere else. Especially in Sarajevo, Bosnian mixed marriages were common between spouses from different faith groups. Often both spouses were observant but each respected the new household's holidays and traditions. Woven into the fabric of society was this ability to co-exist in peace and even overlap into the other's religious space. It was a phenomenon that reminded me of my family and my childhood, when I stood beside my Shiite grandmother in my little *chador* in the morning and then accompanied my parents to a Baha'i holy day celebration in the evening.

Unlike Sarajevo, where I walked by a synagogue, two mosques, a cathedral and an Orthodox church every day on my way to work, Iran's Baha'i properties had always been attacked by the ruling powers who had persecuted followers of the Baha'i Faith since it came into being in 1844. As far back as the 1840s, Baha'is were killed in ways so gruesome that it warranted mention in the reports of foreign ambassadors. Baha'is fired from cannons or tied up with metal rods driven through their hearts or hammered into their flesh by zealots eager to gain a place in heaven. Baha'is driven through the bazaars with candles burning in holes dug out in their flesh.

The only variation over the years was the degree to which the attacks occurred. Iran's Baha'i community was the country's largest religious minority, made up of converts from Islam, Judaism, Zoroastrianism and Christianity. Under the rule of the Shah before the 1979 revolution, Baha'is enjoyed a period of relative freedom from extreme persecution, not counting the villages where random attacks on Baha'i homes and properties never completely came to an end. In my Oakville elementary school, it was mandatory to cover our textbooks with a protective brown paper at the beginning of each school year. My mother told me that it reminded her of buying Baha'i books as a young girl where the old man whose home secretly served as the community bookstore would use the same brown paper to cover the title page of the books to ensure that nobody harassed his customers on their way home.

Growing up, I was aware that I lived in an affluent Toronto suburb that seemed like a parallel reality to the warm country that I had longed for as a child. So many of the people in my childhood memories disappeared or were killed as the Baha'i community, including children, once again became the target for mediaeval-like torture and murder. The day after my grandfather finally left Iran, pressured by my mother, who'd desperately begged him to leave, two bearded revolutionary guards bearing rifles descended on my childhood home to take him for "questioning". I imagined they stood on the same patch of sidewalk where I'd skipped rope with my cousin Taraneh, each of us holding ice cream cones bought from the kiosk across the street. The same patch of sidewalk that I helped the man who worked for us hose down every morning because I loved the smell of wet cement. The guards walked that same patch of sidewalk leading to our door, not knowing that my grandfather had started working in the bazaar at the age of nine to feed his father, brothers and half-sisters. Not knowing that he'd walked that same patch of sidewalk every day on his way to work, holding his cane to steady himself in case of an epileptic tremor. Not knowing that my grandfather had accumulated one of Tehran's most comprehensive personal libraries and taught himself English so he could read the autobiography of Winston Churchill. Not knowing any of this, they appeared at my childhood home based on a list naming enemies of the Islamic Republic.

"*Àgha khooneh neestand,*" they were told at the door. The man of the house is not at home.

"*Kojast?*" they'd asked. Where is he?

"*Raftand kharej.*" He's gone abroad. Abroad, my grandfather died in an Oakville hospital when I was 17, and was buried far from the patch of sidewalk that bore witness to much of his life.

"He's CIA," muttered my Man-Boy after a dinner party to which I'd invited my American boss Tuck, a Danish colleague, and the local staff who worked in our judicial restructuring project.

Postwar Bosnia and Herzegovina was a playground for countries trying to assert supremacy over each other in the world of third-rate international espionage. It was a world confirming that James Bond movies were strictly a figment of somebody's imagination, not at all like the reality of modern-day spying conducted by a bumbling crew of international misfits with accentuated views of themselves playing cloak and dagger in a foreign country. They were easy to spot among the ranks of the "International Community". Narrow-minded, unimaginative, lacking compassion for anyone or anything, they ran projects and worked as managers with no understanding of, or interest in, the people and culture of the country that afforded them a luxury lifestyle they could never have enjoyed at home.

For this dinner, I'd made *adas polo*, a Persian rice dish with raisins and lentils, and *masto khiar,* yoghurt with diced cucumbers sprinkled with dry mint. I had also included a chicken dish, the recipe for which I'd made several very expensive phone calls to my aunt in Amsterdam to perfect. Proud of my Persian dinner and wanting to produce an authentic Persian experience for my guests, I also played my Googoosh CD — beautiful Googoosh was a pre-Revolutionary singer, the symbol of all that was good before the beards.

The American and the Dane arrived first, bearing bottles of wine, clearly for their own enjoyment since they'd ascertained that morning that I didn't drink. I was surprised first by the quantity of the bottles and then by the fact that they'd brought nothing else. In Iranian culture, appearing as a guest empty-handed, *daste-khaly*, advertised your absolute lack of class. Bosnian culture had similar standards and the local guests arrived bearing a cake and a bunch of flowers.

The Street of Good Fortune

Man-Boy helped me serve dinner, which I laid out on the hand-embroidered tablecloth I'd bought from a woman in one of the villages I'd once visited with the UNHCR. "Turn down this music," spat out Tuck, my grimacing boss. "Why is she screeching?"

I stared at him in disbelief and Man-Boy crouched in front of the CD player and turned down my beloved Googoosh, who'd been softly accompanying my domestic activities. The evening did not improve when Tuck insisted on getting drunk with his Scandinavian buddy. "Where's the alcohol we brought?" he bellowed as he picked the lentils and raisins out of the rice with his fingers and asked for bread.

At the end of the evening, in my apartment decorated with empty wine bottles and a platter of *adas polo*, chiefly consumed by my Bosnian guests, I crumpled on the couch and began to cry in the arms of Man-Boy.

"He's CIA, Meri. *To se vidi iz aviona.*" You can see that from an airplane.

I didn't really care what he was. I felt so small, disrespected and humiliated.

"Why are you upset? *To je njihova sramota a ne tvoja.*" It's their shame and not yours, he consoled me.

He cleaned up the bottles and gathered the garbage while I remained slumped on the couch listening to Googoosh and feeling, for the first time I could remember, proud to be Iranian.

11

"Meri, Can I Call You Mama?"

Baka's flat had two rooms and had once housed two families, one in each room; the family of her son with his wife and two children and the other, Baka herself and the three orphaned children of her daughter. By the time I was in the picture Baka lived in her flat alone and served us Turkish coffee in the room separated from the kitchen nook by a grey curtain. The side of the curtain that was Baka's living room had a bookcase with glass doors in which she displayed Christmas cards and pictures of her family. Pictures of Seka and her children, and my Man-Boy and me. Pictures of her brother's family in Australia and even pictures of her family by marriage. Glaringly absent in the tiny flat were pictures of her dead daughter, my Man-Boy's mother.

I asked her about it once. It was before dinner and she was standing in front of me, pouring coffee from the *džezva* in her hand, carefully tipping the thick liquid into my *fildžan*, the tiny coffee cup that stood on a saucer on a small stool at my knees, the same stool upon which my Man-Boy had done his homework as a five-year-old boy.

"Baka, why don't you have Ivana's pictures anywhere?"

She straightened up, still holding the now empty *džezva* and looked me straight in the eye with an expression of stoic defeat:

"*Jer boli Meri, boli,*" she replied. Because it hurts, Meri.

Five years later, on the eve of my long-awaited, storybook return to the land of my inspiration, I decided, in a moment, that I would not visit Baka or Seka despite the fact that the pictures of return hanging in my gallery of dreams featured coffee with Baka and at least a day's visit with my Seka and her family. One day about three weeks before my departure I decided to change the exhibition in my gallery of dreams and took down the pictures that included them. It hurt to do it but the pain was more of a dull, muted feeling, like a passing ache from an old injury triggered only by certain movements, rather than the piercing pain I knew I would face standing at Baka's doorstep and seeing her again, but this time as not mine, not belonging to me, someone to whom I could only be connected through the pictures of a past that was gone, never to return. A past that represented for me an entire lifetime so filled was it with meaning and emotion that I couldn't bear to remember it without the buffer of time and distance. Baka and Seka had to stay there — in the past — so that I could return and come back to my now regular life intact.

The Street of Good Fortune

"I thought we were done with that," IMM commented dryly when I finally worked up the courage to tell him that I was thinking about taking a trip back to Bosnia, backwards down memory lane, back to the place that I thought hung over our heads, the home of all the superlatives I'd ever experienced, the home of my mosts and bests. A place that my new man resented, his competition for my affections, home to Man-Boy and my Plan B.

"I know it's your Plan B, Manteghi — if this doesn't work out between us, you always have Bosnia."

Any mention of things not working out between us struck fear into me because I always saw the end at the beginning. I sat in love waiting for that day with a dread that rumbled under the happy moments, the tender glances, and even the loving acts. A dread that I desperately tried to keep from rising to the surface, reminding me that what I feared most always happened. A dread that I could taste in my mouth, bitter and thick, that sometimes overwhelmed me. I was insanely jealous of his exes, other women he'd been with, laughed with, fought with and finally broken up with. Just like I feared he'd break up with me one day.

A day I saw coming the moment I knew I loved him, wanted to be with him, wanted a future with him. The moment I painted pictures in my head again of a happy life with him living in one of the neighbourhoods we'd frequent on our outings, a quaint little side street of Greek Town or Little Italy; warm, red brick houses mainly home to families where children played outside and grandparents watched from the porch. I pictured myself finally domesticated, cooking something impressive with potatoes, his favourite vegetable, in a kitchen full of shiny, helpful appliances, waiting for him to come home, holding a cocoa-coloured baby on my hip. I pictured us together in a cosy kitchen, at the dinner table, talking like we did every day, the kind of familiar conversation that was often about nothing in particular but gave me a sense of comfort, a sense of being known, a sense of warmth, peppered with laughter and predictable answers. Conversation where the sound of his voice, the look in his eye and the way he turned a phrase all meant things only I could decipher. I pictured us after dinner watching our favourite show with me cuddled up against him or my head in his lap. I pictured us, pictures I could see vividly even without closing my eyes. Pictures that represented my prize, my happy ending, my light at the end of the tunnel, my reward for the pain of disruption that had made my life a story of ups and downs that always singled me out.

But it was a happy ending that was almost too bright, too shiny, and too happy, not to mention rather one-sided, and didn't include IMM in the painting phase, so that, in my psyche, self-preservation kicked in and a Plan B emerged. A plan where I convinced myself a failed relationship with him wouldn't hurt because I could simply return to the life I'd left behind. A whole world of people, emotions and experiences that lived inside me, talked to me, consoled me and loved me, a world to which I could retreat at any time, in any moment. A world that could conjure up in me every possible emotion in a way nothing else could. I told myself this lie the first time he asked me if I was planning to go back to Bosnia when I felt strong enough. Inside I knew I couldn't, knew I wouldn't. I knew that I was now somebody else, no longer the girl with a Christiane Amanpour dream, but a new girl with a new dream. A dream I couldn't see just then but one that would inevitably emerge once I felt strong enough.

"You're going to go back there aren't you?" he'd ask me and I would lie. I'd look at him refusing to give him the satisfaction of knowing that I wasn't going anywhere, that I was just waiting for him to want to be with me enough to ask me not to go anywhere, to stay in Toronto, thinking that it would be a choice I'd have to make.

One day I said, "I have three weeks off in August, I'm thinking of taking a quick trip."

"Where to?"

"Uh, just a quick trip to Bosnia."

I didn't have it in me to tell him that I'd already bought a ticket, already announced my arrival, could already taste the coffee, see the colour of the sun, had already decided which cafés I'd frequent, which friends I would see, and where on the coast I'd spend seven sunny days.

"If you tell me not to go I won't — if you tell me it will change things between us, I'll forget about going and I won't hold it against you. We'll just forget it and go on like this never happened," I offered, not sure what I would do if he actually bit, but almost half-wishing he would. Half-wishing he'd lean towards me with those broad, familiar shoulders in a charcoal grey suit as he'd done on our first semi-date those months ago and ask me not to go, to stay with him, to go somewhere together.

I didn't know what I would have done. I didn't know if I would have given up my return.

The return that had been the reason I woke up every morning during those bald months of chemical hell. The return that had saved me from drowning in a sea of hopelessness when I thought about it on those harsh nights in my girlhood single bed where I lay alone with the cancer, neither of us able to sleep. The return of which I'd made epic movies in my mind full of minarets glowing against dusky skies, lush, wild mountains, emerald rivers and red brick houses, missing façades, adorned with the dried remnants of cement that had oozed out between the bricks. Movies stored in the archives of my mind that switched on when I closed my eyes and remembered the life I'd built on my dream.

"Telling you not to go would be the worst thing I could do. Just go. Go and get it out of your system."

On one hand, I was relieved at this outcome. Maybe this meant that he finally wanted to move forward, to cleanse our relationship of the pasts that haunted us and look towards a future together. But did I really want to get Bosnia out of my system? Like some kind of drug that was bad for me or toxic substance I shouldn't have ingested to begin with? I was afraid of how things would change as we waited together for my departure.

The Street of Good Fortune

It wasn't just my departure that frightened me. What frightened me most was the reality I knew I would be forced to face upon my return. For four years my saving grace had been this world in my head, this parallel reality with nostalgic borders that was my place of refuge, my happy place, my living unreality. A world I'd kept alive on the psychological life support of memory. What would happen once I pulled the plug? Once that world had to live on its own without the halo of nostalgia that blurred the bad and made the good glow in a golden, imaginary wash of light for which the only switch was in my head? No matter what happened in my reality, the sometimes stark reality of everyday Canadian life, I always had a Plan B, a happy place, a world to which, at least in my head, I could always return: my emotional safety net, my Balkan home.

Return was a risk. The risk of losing that fantasy, the risk of having to live in a world in which I wasn't sure I could succeed. Cancer had shattered my illusion of certainty, proving that life held no guarantees. Return might change what I had with IMM. Our relationship had been built on the rocks of our pasts.

"You're going to see the Man-Boy?" he asked me during lunch on a sunny summer afternoon.

I sat across from him on the little terrace of an Italian bistro, my legs crossed, one nestled up against his shin, the only public demonstration of affection he ever allowed me. His obvious insecurity snapped me out of my happy trance. Since announcing my Bosnia trip, things between us had become better than ever before. We saw each other daily and he made extra efforts to be warm and attentive that I welcomed with a sense of disbelief, my heart bursting with happiness, my mind shushing all the doubts and fears that had surrounded our union for so long.

"Of course not," I snapped. "Why would I want to see him?"

I had no intention of seeing him. I had carefully chosen the worlds I did not want to touch during my return and the world of Man-Boy was first on the list. Included in that world was the orphanage, Home and Families, the infamous birthplace of my Bosnian adventure, the only place where I had so desperately wanted to help and where I'd so dismally failed. I was in touch with many of the kids I'd known from the orphanage, including Selma and Fata, Irfan's sisters. When I chatted with Selma online for the first time in years, writing in the little box at the bottom of my Facebook page, I asked her how she was.

"Good", she said. "When are you coming to visit?"

"Soon," I said, "this summer."

"Will you visit me?"

"Of course."

I asked her about her little sister Fata: *"A kako ti je Fata?"*

"They sent her away to another institution."

"Why?" I asked, almost numb.

"*Vratila se kasno u domu.*" She came home after curfew.

"How old is she now?"

The number 11 showed up in the little box.

I asked her if she remembered Irfan, having been only six when he died. Of course she remembered, she said, and she remembered how much I loved him. My heart tightened. I asked her about her older sister, the one who'd run away from the orphanage after Irfan's death, the one we tried so hard to find but never did.

"Did you ever see her again?"

No, she hadn't, she said, she never saw her again.

I asked her if her mother or father ever visited her.

"No," she said, "never."

The little window was blank for many minutes. I waited, not wanting to barrage her with more questions, answers to which rehashed the unimaginable sadness of her young life. I saw the little sign appear at the top left-hand corner of the window, meaning that she was writing, and then I saw a question pop up on the screen that stabbed me in the tender underbelly of my emotional anatomy, a place that I'd shut off since Irfan's death and a place I'd worked hard to forget all the while missing its existence in my post-Bosnia, post-cancer world.

"Meri, can I call you Mama?"

Something wrapped itself around my heart and squeezed so hard that I had to fight to breathe. I saw a tidal wave of emotion coming at me. A sudden, unanticipated rush of the feelings I'd buried, the scenes I'd chosen to forget and the heartbreak I'd hidden behind the moments spent with the children, frustrated and defeated, lamenting their circumstances, my heart twitching every time I walked up to the building adorned with a golden plaque, "Home and Families" engraved in its centre. They were words that made me wince when I saw them, words that veiled a reality so opposed to their meaning that it was like some sick individual in the municipality had come up with the name in a moment of sadistic pleasure. When I walked up to the building, five rows of balconies jutted out into the alley displaying little shirts, pants and dresses drying on the clothes lines that hung in each "family's" balcony. Mismatched and faded, little tops and skirts that had been worn by too many children and washed too many times looking sad and tired hanging there, waving in the wind, as if they had somehow taken on the feelings of their tiny wearers. Selma's question waited in the little box for an answer.

For some time I'd followed Selma and Fata's pictures, my heart heavy when I saw how much they'd grown and how different they looked now from the last time I'd seen them, reminding me that I'd been absent from their lives for too long. I was weighed down by the guilt I felt when I thought about them. The guilt I felt for having abandoned them, first when Irfan died, and again when I looked at their pictures and realised that despite my best intentions for them, my zigzag of emotions about them and the hope I had given them, I hadn't improved their lives.

Call me Mama?

What kind of mama had I ever been to her? But there it was, in black and white, the question that stared at me on the computer screen, "Meri, can I call you Mama?" waiting for a response. I felt so guilty saying yes, having made none of the sacrifices that defined motherhood, having given up on them after losing Irfan. But how could I say no? I knew she was there, at the computer in the orphanage, a line of other kids waiting behind her, anxiously staring at the little box on her screen for an answer that was taking too long to be written. I realised that even just the words were enough for her.

"*Naravno sine, ma naravno, volim vas puno i voljela sam ti brata puno.*" Of course *sine*, of course, I love you and I loved your brother so much, and logged out of Facebook without waiting for an answer.

"Don't suffer, don't help anybody," a friend told me, calling right before my trip. "Just go to have a good time — enjoy yourself. Remember that your health comes first."

My health was something I thought about infinitely less as I left my cancer farther behind me. So far, four years from my first round of chemo, my checkups had been routine appointments which I actually enjoyed, dressing up and doing my now waist-length hair as a kind of homage to my doctors, compensating for all the times they saw me sick and bald and too tired and cranky to show how I felt about the care they gave me. So checkups were fun little moments where the nurses and technicians would gush when they saw me, thrilled at how my hair had grown and how peppy I was when I wasn't battling a life-threatening illness. I'd recently been for an MRI at Princess Margaret Hospital where my friend Nava and I made a day of it, going for lunch in a little café behind the hospital that had once been a kosher butcher shop and still displayed remnants of Hebrew writing on its window. This had become a yearly pilgrimage; Nava always accompanied me to MRI appointments and then to other explorations of the downtown core of the city I'd finally begun to think of as home.

This year, the year of my return, the year I was finally strong enough to make my trip back into my dream world, I didn't think twice when I went for my checkup alone, more excited than ever, with a love story in the making and a trip that for me was the ultimate reflection of my survival. The post-MRI checkup had been scheduled the day before my flight and I was late, having scrambled to shop and pack.

"We saw something in your right breast. We don't think it's significant but we need to do an ultrasound to make sure. It's been scheduled for next week."

It took two seconds for the words to make sense and then I reeled in shock. The room began to spin and I doubled over, hyperventilating, making no attempt to veil my distress. What I feared most, more than anything, was happening. Disbelief and then soul-gripping fear swirled inside me and the only thought that repeated itself over and over again in my head came out of my mouth between sobs and gasps for breath.

"I can't do it again, I can't do it again."

In one split second, my trip, my breast, my life, were all hanging in the balance and I couldn't separate them into manageable compartments without help. Distraught and terrified, I racked my brain about what I should do and whom I should dial. I called my man. "He's with a client," his assistant told me, "do you want me to call him out?" she asked in response to the obvious anxiety in my tone. "No, no, it's fine." I hung up and dialled home. "This is 905-847-9689 we cannot take your call at this time…" droned the voicemail.

I called the one person who could understand me and she answered, "Hey, babe," in her soft, light voice.

"Beks, I have to cancel my trip," I heaved into the phone, my voice a sob.

"Calm down and tell me what's going on."

Beks and I kept each other up to date on our checkups and MRI appointments and she knew exactly where I was. "Good luck babe," she'd called to say that morning.

"OK, calm down. You have to calm down."

But I couldn't. All I could think was how could this be happening to me again? What had I done wrong? Perhaps it was all the food I'd eaten in restaurants, un-organic and teeming with hormones and preservatives. Perhaps I'd eaten too much red meat or not enough fruits and vegetables as recommended to post-cancer patients. Oh God, I should have made myself vegetable juice every morning like I had during my recovery, full of beets, carrots and celery as prescribed by the myriad natural healing sources my parents had uncovered over the course of my illness. I should have grown my own wheatgrass to juice, as exhorted by the cleansing centre where I'd vowed to maintain an organic, vegan lifestyle. I thought back to all the burgers and coffees and toxins I'd happily consumed, knowing that I was violating the laws of naturopathy, homeopathy and healthy living but exhilarated by the feeling that I was now a normal person, not sick, no longer sick, and able to live in moments where I wasn't constantly reminded of the cancer. After our treatments ended, Beks and I had spent three weeks in a detox facility in San Diego, on an organic, vegan diet complete with wheatgrass juice enemas. Having thoroughly cleansed my colon and calmed my mind in the daily yoga classes, I felt new and improved, as I'd done everything possible to ensure that this was the last I'd see of cancer.

"Let me make some calls," said Beks after I tearfully explained everything.

My next dial, a hysterical call, was my ultimate, definitive test of my man's, character. A test I'd always wondered about but could hardly wish upon myself. What would he do now? How would he react? Would he fail me or would he come through? Would he erase the memory of how I'd been let down by a Bosnian Man-Boy and win a bright, shining spot at the top of the love podium, or would he, too, fall by the wayside, confirming my already tainted opinion of men when faced with a crisis? The time we'd spent together, the lunches and outings, the compliments and tender moments shared all disappeared in the face of one single event.

"You don't know anything yet, Manteghi. If they say it's insignificant then it's probably nothing. Don't assume the worst."

Don't assume the worst? I could only assume the worst. It hurt me that he didn't spring into action, shut down his office, and make his way to be by my side, that my hysteria invoked in him logic and reason and not emotion, which to me was the right reaction, the only reaction.

"That's all you can say to me right now?" I shrieked into the phone.

"Manteghi, I'm stressed, I had non-stop clients today and I just don't need all this drama."

I thought back to my trip with Beks at the detox facility, where we took daily power walks during which we rehashed our pre-cancer relationships.

"Babe, imagine you'd met a guy who'd been there for you the whole time during cancer, losing your hair, maybe losing your fertility. A guy who would have been kind and supportive through all of it?"

"Without cheating?" I fantasised.

"Yeah", she chuckled, "without cheating."

I imagined a cross between my father and Dr. Verma.

"Imagine how lucky a guy like that would be now. Imagine how much you'd love a guy like that. Just imagine."

As much as I tried, I didn't have that wild an imagination.

But with the advent of a new man, my imagination had softened and expanded. Sometimes, looking at him across the table, I wondered how he would have reacted if he'd seen me while I was in the throes of treatment. I wondered if those eyes that looked at me now with appreciation and desire would have looked away if they'd seen me on the street or in a store during my extraterrestrial phase.

My life with cancer flashed before my eyes; the day in the shower when I'd offered clump after clump of hair at the altar of a red toxic substance that burned through my veins and destroyed the old me so that a new me could live. The day I sat in our green and white kitchen in front of the unusually placed mirror on one of its walls submitting silently to my father's black clippers as they grazed my scalp transforming me into a shell of the girl I'd been only a week before. The months I'd spent agonising over my fertility, my ovaries, my period, and the very slow return of my eyelashes and eyebrows. The years it took me to *dodjem sebi*, come back to myself, after the experience of beating a chance mutation that nearly took my life. The years struggling with the choices I'd made, all of which had led me to dead ends, I believed. The years I spent getting my life back together in a country where I felt I didn't belong. The nights I wondered if my life before cancer had been a series of mistakes, miscalculations based on naïve assumptions. It was too much, too cruel, too unfair to ask me to do it all again, made more horrific since I already knew how everything went.

Beks, as usual, came through with the calm, steady focus under pressure that I'd always admired in her, especially while we were sick.

"My brother got you in for an ultrasound today. Go right now and tell them Dr. Sharif sent you."

Beks's brother was senior radiologist at a Toronto hospital and had managed to contact his colleague at Princess Margaret, who agreed to squeeze me into their ultrasound schedule that day.

"Looks like you're just not destined to ever go back there," sighed Holly when I called her from the hospital to inform her about what had happened. I had struggled to make peace with bad things happening, a fact of life I realised nobody, in the long run, could escape but I still harboured a sense of entitlement, that having survived cancer and spent years recovering from it physically and emotionally, the universe owed me a happy ending. This was clearly not it.

When Nava and I went to the Princess Margaret, she was so familiar with the hospital that she led the way, walking through the corridors that ended in the women-only waiting room where I waited, dressed in two blue hospital gowns, one covering my naked back and the other covering my breasts, my life's constant frenemies, still perky and firm in halter dresses and bikinis, the masters of my fate, deciding everything from whether I could travel to whether I would live. Other women dressed in the same blue gowns sat in the waiting room and one by one their names were called. Nava sat beside me, her personality distracting me from the reality of where I was. My name was called.

"Can she come in with me?" I asked the nurse. Nava, not waiting for a reply, walked into the room and beckoned me in.

"Come on then," she said in her posh London accent and I obeyed, as did the nurse who possibly believed that Nava might be Princess Margaret herself.

I lay on the bed and Nava sat at my feet as the doctor covered my breast with a dark blue cloth with a square window cut out in the fabric. She squeezed the familiar clear gel onto my exposed skin and began to search around my right breast, looking over at the image that had triggered the day's events on the screen beside her.

As her hand manoeuvred the ultrasound in short, firm sweeps across my breast, I could only think of the last time I lay on a hospital bed when the doctor gasped as she guided the machine across my breast. "How long has this been here?" she'd asked incredulously and I couldn't stand to remember what happened after that while I waited to know whether it would be happening again. I exploded into tears, gasping for breath as I sobbed through the procedure, unable to control myself, unable to stop.

The doctor, a slim, attractive woman in her late thirties with a Spanish accent, comforted me.

"There's nothing, there's nothing there, it's nothing, I know you had a bad experience but there's nothing, it's OK, we just had to make sure."

But I couldn't stop and as she patted my hand, sympathetic to my feelings, her colleague, a bald doctor with round, gold rimmed glasses came into the room and surveyed the scene with a puzzled look.

"You are going to Yugoslavia?" he asked in a thick Russian accent.

"Yes," I blubbered, wiping my nose on my hand. He stepped to one side, a move that opened the path between me and the door and, offering me a box of Kleenex, nodded towards the exit.

"Have a good trip."

The plane began its descent into my valley surrounded by mountains and enveloped in the mist that made landing in

Sarajevo impossible during the winter months. It was August, though, and the bright summer sun shone over the red rooftops of my city, clusters of houses and villages nestled into the green dips. I saw the crooked black line that divided the lush landscape and recognised the Miljačka, the only one of Bosnia's rivers that ran through Sarajevo, dividing it and making it necessary for a series of bridges to be built along its length, connecting its halves. The sun shone with the exact intensity I remembered; the green that covered the mountains was just as vivid as when I'd fallen in love with it and the houses stood on their foundations, still so many façadeless, in mid-construction. As I disembarked from the tiny Lufthansa plane onto Sarajevo airport's runway, I began to miss the city as soon as my feet touched the ground, knowing that this was just a visit and not a return home like all the other times I'd landed there before. Knowing that too soon I would be back on this runway, back on a plane, on my way back to the destiny I'd struggled against at any cost.

In response to this knowledge I drank in every scene and every moment, every look and every word directed at me by the customs officer who stamped my passport.

"*Dobrodošli.*" Welcome.

He handed me back my passport and I peered into his face, wondering if he'd worked here before during my previous life, where I took that welcome for granted so many times, never guessing that one day that word uttered mechanically by a burly Bosnian customs officer who scratched his head under his hat would move me to tears. You don't know how long I've been waiting to hear that, I wanted to tell him. From you, exactly at this moment, exactly like this, exactly how I'd imagined for four long years.

I walked into the baggage claims area and it was exactly the same as when I'd left. The same European diaspora flown in on their annual trips home waiting for their luggage and talking loudly on cell phones with the family that waited for them behind the sliding door that led to the arrivals area and then to the city, that city. I waited impatiently for my black bag with wheels on the bottom. Even though I hadn't slept for 17 hours and had changed planes three times before arriving in Sarajevo at 11 am, I was awake, alert, and full of adrenaline. My bag appeared and as it made its way slowly around the carousel, I prepared to grab it and get past the sliding doors. I heaved my bag off the track, slid up the handle and began to roll it towards the exit. I was so nervous and walked so quickly that the bag tipped over several times.

The doors slid back and I walked slowly forward, taking in the sight of the arrivals hall full of people waiting. Before I could begin to search for a face, Olja was embracing me with one hand, grabbing my bag with the other.

"*Izgledaš ko mina, ko mina Meri!*" You look so good, Meri!

I hadn't seen Olja since the day she'd visited me in the hospital during my bout of post-chemo illness. I'd been quarantined while the doctors worked to find out what exactly what was wrong with me and there was a tray with masks and gowns outside of my room that my doctors and visitors would put on before entering. She'd refused the gown and mask the nurse had urged her to wear. When the nurse protested, Olja gave her a look of disdain, kissed me on the cheek, and loudly declared, "I survived the siege of Sarajevo – I don't need a gown".

The new me had hair down to my waist again and was thinner than the girl who'd left Sarajevo. This was mostly due to a daily pre-Sarajevo running regimen that I had established to ensure that I could walk amongst Sarajevo girls with my head held high and, also, accompany several of them to the coast in bikinis that Bosnian girls rocked like no women I'd ever seen. Olja looked me up and down with a big smile on her face and asked me where I wanted to go.

"*U gradu,*" I answered. "Downtown."

She rolled my bag out of the arrivals hall and towards the row of taxis that waited. A driver got out of his seat to put my bag in the trunk: it was all I could do not to jump into his arms and hug him. A Sarajevo taxi driver! Such a key role in the movies in my head. I sat in front with him while Olja sat in the back and gave directions. As the taxi pulled out of the airport and drove down the road leading to the city, I rolled down the window, stuck my head out and breathed in the sun, the smog, and the dust that rose as the taxi made its way closer and closer to the city.

"*Ona je godinama čekala da se vrati,*" Olja explained to the driver, who was so puzzled he forgot to ask if she or I were married. She's waited for years to return here.

The Street of Good Fortune

"*Od rata?*"

Since the war? he asked, thinking I was of the diaspora who'd left in the war.

"*Ne, od kad je se razboljela.*" No, since she got sick, Olja responded, and the driver, noticing that Olja and I were speaking to each other in English, asked her, "*Odakle je?*" Where is she from?" Before she could say anything I answered, "*Odavdje, Ja sam Sarajka,*" I'm from here, I'm a Sarajevo girl.

There she was waiting for me, as if I'd never left. Still the city I remembered. Still the city I loved. My beloved, beleaguered Sarajevo. My city of a thousand smiles and a thousand stories. My city of sadness, joy, and revival, my revival from the unawakened state in which I'd been before I went there; I'd come back to her so she could revive me again, after being forced to leave her with a cancer that was now healed, I'd come back for her to heal my soul.

I walked down Ferhadija, the pedestrian stretch that led to the Old Town and Pigeon Square and the mosque with the roses. I ran to the big wooden door of the mosque with brass handles set in the stone wall and peeked into the courtyard, looking for the roses I remembered, the roses I used to pass by every day on my way to work. They were still there, the roses, red and yellow flashes of colour against the green garden that adorned the entrance to the mosque. We sat in Pigeon Square, Olja and I, and ordered *fildžan* after *fildžan* of Turkish coffee and *zova*, a sweet, cold drink made of elderberries. I closed my eyes, savouring every sip of coffee, every conversation of every passerby, every sound and syllable of the language in which I was now enveloped and let myself fall back into Sarajevo, back into the mould of the girl who'd had no fear, who'd forged a new life in an old country and made it her own. I sat watching the pigeons, talking to Olja and biting into a pink square of Turkish delight in a scene that could have suited a postcard. The city lived around me, waiters bustled between chairs and shooed away shameless pigeons that landed on empty café tables. The same city that gave me life and then nearly took it away. The same city that watched me as I watched her, from afar, waiting and hoping for a day when we would again come face to face. The same city whose streets I'd walked a thousand times in my memory bursting with the emotions I knew I would feel when I would be there again, but this time not in memory, this time in full, multi-dimensional reality. A reality I could hardly believe I was living. A reality that had been a dream I clung to with all of my being for four long years knowing only that I had to reach it. Small groups of middle-aged men walked together towards the mosque as I heard the call to prayer, soft and beautiful and half of me, the half I'd numbed, then forgotten, came out of its deep slumber, kissed by the city I loved.

About the Author

MARYAM MANTEGHI'S WORDS touched me for the first time when a mutual friend 'liked' her status update on Facebook. I expressed my sincere appreciation for her talent and ability to communicate what most people would deeply relate to but have a hard time articulating. Hours later we exchanged a few private messages and what followed were a welter of emails and phone calls that created a bond of friendship and sisterhood. I happened to be in the right place at the right time and offered to publish her book.

By heritage and conviction a Baha'i, Maryam's ethnic mix includes Jewish, Persian and Kurdish. She's fluent in English, French and Farsi and competent in Bosnian. A graduate of the University of Toronto and the University of Windsor, she also studied human rights law at Oxford. She's practiced immigration law in Canada, worked for United Nations organisations in Bosnia and Herzegovina and clerked in The Hague, the Netherlands with the International Tribunal of the Former Yugoslavia. She currently runs her own law firm.

Leyla T. Haidarian
Forefront Media Group

www.ingramcontent.com/pod-product-compliance
Lightning Source LLC
Chambersburg PA
CBHW031640040426
42453CB00006B/163